INSIGHT POCKET GUIDES

FIJI
Islands

APA PUBLICATIONS

Part of the Langenscheidt Publishing Group

L

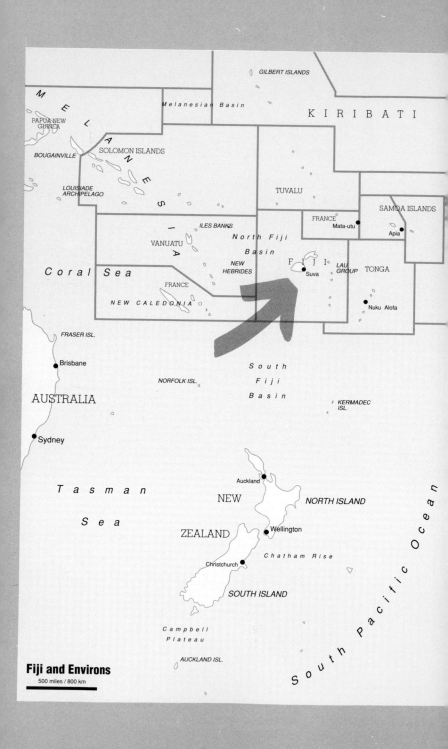

Fiji and Environs

500 miles / 800 km

Welcome!

Dazzling white sand beaches, brilliant turquoise-blue waters, rustic villages and time-forgotten townships. Fiji's bejewelled islands offer all these and more. Much has changed since the tourist industry first took off in the early 1960s, but happily not the Fijian people whose friendliness and hospitality is legendary. Though tourism has developed, it is still minuscule compared to other places. There are no gigantic hotels; many resorts are family owned and managed, and offer the kind of intimacy impossible to experience elsewhere. Here, you are not a cipher to be processed and sent home again but a special guest to be looked after and honoured. This is what makes Fiji special.

 James Siers, writer, filmmaker and adventurer, first came to Fiji in 1962 on a photo-journalism assignment. He was captivated by the striking scenery, the gracious people and Fiji's romantic past. 'In the 30 years since that first visit,' Siers recalls, 'I became a frequent visitor, to write and photograph several books on the islands as well as to direct films. After returning almost every year, in 1984 I decided this was the place I would settle in.'

Siers starts off with three full-day itineraries which quickly introduce you to the varied attractions on the main island of Viti Levu. A series of *Pick & Mix* options, in and outside Viti Levu, offer more leisurely diversions while those with more time on their hands are invited to venture further afield with the *Excursions* section. Here are suggestions for visits to the outer islands, village stays, hikes to the jungle-clad interiors, exclusive resorts and luxury cruises, and diving and deep sea fishing trips. Select as few or as many of the itineraries as you wish. Together, they represent the best of what Fiji's 300 islands have to offer.

C O N T E N T S

Pages 2/3:
Yachts at anchor,
Mamanutha Islands

Excursions

The following six excursions are ideal for visitors with more time. They range from two days to a week or more and cover a range of activities and a spectrum of Fijian islands.

Pages 8/9: Smiling Fijian youngsters

HISTORY

Fiji's human history began sometime around the year 1500BC. There is no evidence as to who those first settlers were. Items unearthed in burial sites and archaeological excavations show that they were of the same stock as those who later became the Polynesians of Tonga, Samoa and the major islands of the east: Tahiti, Hawaii, the Marquesas, Tuamotus, Gambiers, Austral Islands, Easter Island and New Zealand.

Various theories postulate that the first settlers lived in Fiji for more than 1,000 years after its discovery, co-existing with later migrants in a state of war and peace. During this process, the people we recognise today as Polynesian gradually moved to eastern Fiji, the Lau Islands and Tonga until finally the Fijians as we know them today became dominant over the entire group of islands.

Point of Origin

The undoubted point of origin was Southeast Asia which includes Indonesia, the Philippines, Borneo and Papua New Guinea. Human habitation of New Guinea has now been established to have occurred more than 40,000 years ago. At a later date, new migrants began to move down and at some point, now thought to have been 5,000 years ago, a maritime culture established itself in New Ireland and New Britain and then quickly moved down through the Solomon Islands to Vanuatu, New Caledonia and Fiji and on to Tonga, Samoa, the Marquesas, Tahiti, Hawaii and New Zealand. This achievement ranks them as the greatest sailors the world has ever known.

Those early sailors who fearlessly roamed the Pacific Ocean are

A communal gathering outside a Fijian bure

Early bare-breasted Fijian beauties

today referred to as the Lapita because of a distinct style of pottery first discovered in 1952 at a site in New Caledonia of the same name. Pottery remains discovered in Marquesas tell an interesting story: the material used for grouting came from the Rewa River delta on the island of Viti Levu in Fiji. This points to trading links between the people of Tonga and Fiji and to active voyaging from Tonga to Samoa and the east.

Scientists working with the tools of archaeology, linguistics and botany are still trying to piece together what really might have happened but enough has been revealed for a comprehensive outline. The Lapita discover and settle Fiji sometime before 1500BC. Within a short time of their settlement, some continue with exploratory voyages to Tonga, Samoa and then the major islands of east Polynesia. The remaining population increases and war once again becomes endemic. New migrants arrive from the west and human bones are discovered in middens, along with those of animals and other foodstuffs. Cannibalism becomes part of life. Fiji enters a period of intense political rivalry which exists up to the time of European contact. Some aspects of Melanesian culture are retained but the material and social culture is principally Polynesian.

European Contact

In 1643, Dutch navigator Abel Tasman sailed to the north-east of Fiji. The reef which was nearly his ruin bears the name Heemskirk, after one of his ships. Tasman sighted the islands of Taveuni, Qamea, Laucala, Rabi and part of Vanua Levu, but he did not pause to examine his discovery. Captain James Cook was next in 1774. He laid off the island of Vatoa in southern Lau, left some trinkets ashore and continued to the west without realising the extent of the archipelago.

The true extent of Fiji was not discovered until 1789 when Captain William Bligh sailed through the entire group after being set adrift in Tonga by the mutineers who seized the HMS *Bounty*. Bligh passed through a portion of Lau in eastern Fiji and then between Koro and Wakaya, within easy distance of Ovalau and through the Vatu i Ra channel which divides Viti Levu from Vanua Levu. He went on past Yasawa i Rara at the north-western extremity, thus

Fijian outrigger canoe

leaving Fiji behind. A large canoe was launched by the Fijians in pursuit from Yasawa i Rara and came within bow shot of Bligh and his men. Several arrows were fired but Bligh and his men managed to escape. The large, reef-strewn body of water between the north-western coast of Viti Levu, the Yasawa Islands and the Mamanutha Islands is to this day known as Bligh Water.

Cannibalism

Europeans who ventured to Fiji before the turn of the century confirmed stories told in Tonga of hazardous reefs and the duplicity of the people and their cannibal appetites. In 1794, the captain of the American brig *Arthur* had to defend his ship with musket and cannon against the natives. During the course of the next 50 years, less cautious captains would lose their vessels. These hazards were sufficient to deter casual traffic, but when sandalwood was discovered it offered sufficient incentive to overlook both the dangers. This period in Fiji's history began just after the turn of the century and ended some 10 years later but it was to have a profound effect on the Fijian people, and their culture and politics.

The most important effect was the introduction of the gun and its unscrupulous use by shipwrecked mercenaries, the most significant of whom was Charlie Savage, a Swede. Coupled with the policy of an ambitious chief on the small island of Bau, the weapons proved decisive in war and helped elevate Bau to a state of pre-eminence which it enjoys to this day.

Savage was rewarded with many wives from well-born families; the male issue of which were strangled at birth so as not to complicate future succession claims. He was regarded with dread and awe by most Fijians. His reputation, however, was not sufficient to save his life during a skirmish in Vanua Levu following a dispute. Savage, who went to parley with the opposing side, was drowned by having his head immersed in a pool of water and then dismembered, cooked and eaten before his friends. The episode ended less dramatically so for his friends: they managed to seize the head priest as hostage and were thus able to get to safety.

Levuka – the old capital in the 19th century

New Trade

Ten years after the demise of the sandalwood trade, a new trade began for *beche de mer* (sea cucumber) in the 1820s. As with sandalwood, a fortune could be made and this was enough to bring many ships to Fiji where they became embroiled in local conflicts. By now Fiji also had a resident population of European beachcombers. Some like Charlie Savage were shipwrecked castaways; others had jumped ship; some like William Lockerby and David Whippy had been left on the beach because of conflict with their superior officers. Yet others came to seek their fortunes in trade.

The natural centre for these men was Levuka, on the island of Ovalau, where the prevailing east-south-east wind made it easy for sailing ships to enter and leave port. Levuka was also in close proximity to the centres of power at Bau and Rewa and the most populous parts of Fiji. Some of these men gained fortunes. The American David Whippy, whose descendants number more than 1,000 today, is a good example. Left ashore by his elder brother, he at first became a mercenary, rose to be trusted ambassador to the state of Bau and later became appointed the American consul for Fiji. Later, he acquired 9,000 acres of land at Wainunu in Vanua Levu, and established a shipyard (which was operated until 1990 by his descendants) and died an honoured man.

At the time of European contact, the relatively new state of Bau was on the ascent against its neighbours, the ancient and most powerful states of Verata and Rewa. Cakaudrove, which controlled a large part of Vanua Levu, Taveuni and its associated smaller islands, was also in contention but eventually, as did the others, acknowledged Bau as pre-eminent.

Conversion to Christianity

A new consideration was the arrival of Tongan chief Ma'afu in Fiji in 1840 who came close to winning control of the entire Fijian group. He was thwarted in his ambition by the cession of Fiji to Britain by leading chiefs in 1874. The importance of Wesleyan missionaries who arrived in 1835 from Tonga cannot be overlooked in this equation because it was the 1853 conversion of Seru Cakobau, the Vunivalu (chief) of Bau, and decisive Tongan intervention in a war between Cakobau and others which finally ended the chapter on old Fiji. Cakobau's conversion to Christianity also brought about the conversion of most of the population.

Cession to Britain

The inability of Cakobau to form an effective government in the 1870s caused a crisis of a magnitude which could not be resolved. The ever more threatening Tongan presence, directed by the able Ma'afu was poised to swallow Fiji as a colony of Tonga and gave added impetus for the Bauan chief and other leading chiefs to cede the islands to Britain in 1874.

The cession of Fiji encouraged a new wave of European settlers. A plantation society which grew and processed coconuts into oil was developed in the 1840s and began to thrive. Only the lack of cheap, reliable labour held it in check. A stop had been put to 'black birding' – a practice nothing short of slavery – just prior to cession. Islanders in the Solomons and Vanuatu were lured aboard 'recruiting' ships with promises of trade goods and then abducted to be contracted to plantation owners in Fiji.

The planting and processing of sugar cane made it imperative to have a large supply of cheap labour and so the colonial administration made the decision to recruit indentured labour from India on 5-year contracts. The first contingent arrived in 1878 and the system was to continue until 1916. By this time, Fiji's sugar industry was controlled by the Australian Colonial Sugar Refining Company. As the company could not survive without the Indians, a government decision was made to allow those who wished to stay in Fiji to do so, despite protests from the Great Council of (Fijian) Chiefs. Most chose to remain and by 1970, when Fiji became independent, Indians outnumbered native Fijians in a total population of over 700,000.

Ratu Seru Cakabau

Military Coups

In 1987, a coalition between the Indians and Fijians won the general election and provoked two (bloodless) military coups by the army which was almost entirely composed of Fijian troops. A new constitution was pro-

Fijian entertainment

mulgated which gave Fijians a guaranteed majority in government. In 1992, 5 years after the coups, a general election was held. The man who had engineered the coups, Major General Sitiveni Rabuka, became the Prime Minister of a coalition comprising members of his own Fijian party sponsored by the chiefs and that of the general electors who represented people of European, part-European, Chinese, part-Chinese and of Pacific Island origin. Two parties representing the Indian community formed the opposition and have been agitating for a review of the constitution which divides the electorate on racial grounds. It has been agreed that a review will take place.

Fijian Culture

The essential nature of Fijian culture survives to this day, due to as much to its strengths as to its relative isolation until recently from the rest of the world.

About 90 percent of Fijians still live in villages in the countryside and the power of the *vanua* − one's land and family ties − is still the most powerful cultural force. Extended family units known as *matagali* comprise village communities who own land in common. The concept of individual ownership is foreign in a village where everything is shared and the word *kerekere* means a request that cannot be denied.

In practice, Fijians who live in cities and are faced with expenditure for rent, food and clothing find it difficult to cope with requests from relatives who arrive, expecting to be housed, fed and clothed without concern as to who will pay for it. The problem is magnified when a Fijian ventures into business. If he has a store and a distant relative without money wants to buy something, he cannot refuse, knowing full well the account will never be settled.

Each village has a chief who in turn owes allegiance to a higher chief. Paramount chiefs represent former political states and command the highest respect. They comprise the Bose Levu Vaka Turaga (The Great Council of Chiefs) whose deliberations and decisions are held by some to be more important than those of parliament. These are men descended from the chiefs who ceded Fiji to Britain in 1874, and who now claim the right of their ancestors to supreme authority in independent Fiji.

The other half of Fiji's population comprises the descendants of Indian indentured labourers who began arriving in the country in 1878. By scraping and saving, and hard work and investment, some have prospered beyond belief. This is often a sore point with many Fijians who want to maintain political control until such time they have reached economic parity, a concept which many consider impossible to achieve without a cultural revolution.

Historical Highlights

1736BC Revealed by archaeology as the earliest settlement date.

1643AD Abel Tasman sights the north-eastern islands of Taveuni. Ships *Heemskercq* and *Zeehaen* strike and cross Heemskirk Reef with only slight damage.

1774 James Cook sights and lands at Vatoa Island in southern Lau.

1789 William Bligh sails through the islands in his ship's launch after the mutiny on HMS *Bounty* in Tonga.

1792 Bligh returns in the vessel, HMS *Providence*.

1797 The London Missionary Society's ship *Duff* enters Fiji from the north and strikes Heemskirk Reef.

1799 American merchant ship *Ann* and *Hope* sail through Fiji.

1800 American schooner *Argo* is wrecked in Lau. Surviving crew bring a devastating epidemic. This kills thousands of Fijians.

1804 Olive Slater discovers sandalwood in Vanua Levu and is responsible for the sandalwood trade until the logs are depleted in 1814 which brings about great changes in Fiji.

1820 Marks the start of the *beche de mer* trade of cured sea slugs dominated by American ships from Salem, New England.

1820–60 British and Yankee ships hunt sperm and humpback whales in Fijian waters and sign on Fijians as crew.

1825 London Missionary Society attempts to establish mission but catechists remain in Tonga.

1830 Second attempt to set up mission fails after three Tahitian catechists are given a hostile reception.

1835 Wesleyan Missionaries David Cargill and William Cross arrive from Tonga and establish at Lau.

1865 First attempt to form a Fiji confederacy as an experiment in a unified government fails

1867 The Tongan Chief Ma'afu forms the Northern Confederacy with some success.

1870 'Black birding', the kidnapping of people from other South Pacific Islands for cheap labour in Fiji, is brought to an end.

1871 Ratu Seru Cakobau, the Vunivalu of Bau, declares himself the Tui Viti (King of Fiji) and forms a government at Levuka which survives for 3 years. Start of the Colo wars.

1874 Fiji ceded to Britain. Measles epidemic begins and eventually claims 40,000 Fijians.

1877 Suva is the new capital.

1879 Indentured labour from India is introduced to provide labour on plantations.

1880 Development of sugar cane growing and processing industry.

1881 Rotuma becomes part of the Colony of Fiji.

1888 Birth of Ratu Sir Lala Sukuna, high chief, scholar and soldier of distinction in the 1914 Great War. Ratu Sukuna awarded Medaille Militaire for bravery while serving with the French Foreign Legion on the Western Front.

1919 Indenture system ends officially. Most Indians decide to remain in the Fiji islands.

1928 Kingsford Smith arrives from Hawaii and lands at Albert Park on an epic transpacific flight.

1932 Gold discovered at Mt Kasi, Savusavu, and Tavua in Viti Levu, where it is still mined today.

1939 World War II.

1942 Japanese occupy Banaba (Ocean Island); Fijians enlist and serve with distinction with the Allied forces in the Solomon Islands.

1952 Fijian troops leave for anti communist campaigns in Malaysia.

1958 Death of Ratu Sir Lala Sukuna.

1970 Fiji becomes independent after 96 years of British rule.

1987 Two military coups against a coalition Government of Fijians and Indians. Formation of an interim administration.

1992 General elections under a new constitution guarantees ethnic Fijians a majority of seats in the Upper and Lower Houses of Parliament. Prime Minister announces that the constitution will be reviewed by a bipartisan commission.

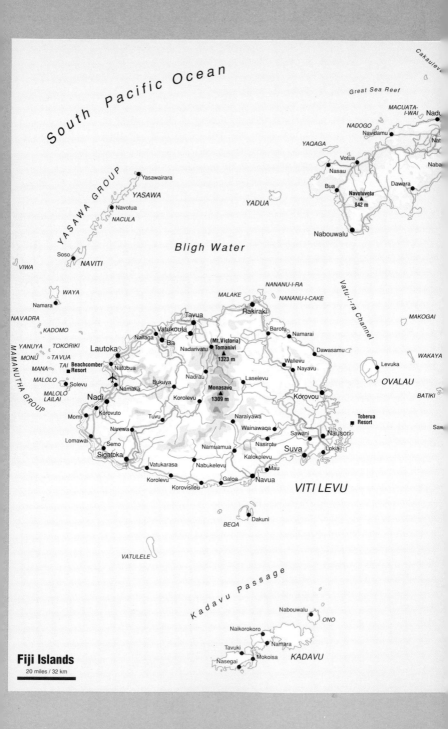

South Pacific Ocean

Cakaulevu

Great Sea Reef

MACUATA-
I-WAI   Nadi

NADOGO
Navidamu   Nati

YAQAGA
Votua   Naba
Nasau

Bua
Dawara
Navotuvotu
842 m

Nabouwalu

YASAWA GROUP

Yasawairara

YASAWA

Navotua

NACULA

YADUA

Bligh Water

Soso

VIWA   NAVITI

WAYA

NANANU-I-RA

MAKOGAI

Namara

MALAKE

NANANU-I-CAKE

NAVADRA

KADOMO

Rakiraki

Vatu-i-ra Channel

YANUYA   TOKORIKI

Tavua

Barotu

WAKAYA

MONŪ   TAVUA

Lautoka

Vatukoula

Namarai

MANA   TAI

Nailaga   Ba

(Mt. Victoria)
Tomanivi
1323 m

Dawasamu

Levuka

MALOLO

Beachcomber
Resort

Natubua

Nadarivatu

Wallevu

OVALAU

MALOLO
LAILAI

Solevu

Bukuya

Nadrau

Nayavu

BATIKI

Nadi

Namaka

Laselevu

Momi

Korovuto

Korolevu

Monasavo
1309 m

Korovou

Saw

Tuvu

Narewa

Narayawa

Toberua
Resort

Lomawai

Semo

Wainawaqa

Sawani

Nausori

Sigatoka

Namuamua

Nasirotu

Suva

Lokia

Vatukarasa

Nabukelevu

Kalokolevu

Korolevu

Galoa

Mau

Korovisilou

Navua

VITI LEVU

Dakuni

BEQA

VATULELE

Kadavu Passage

Nabouwalu

ONO

Naikorokoro

Namara

Tavuki

Nasegai   Mokoisa

KADAVU

Fiji Islands

20 miles / 32 km

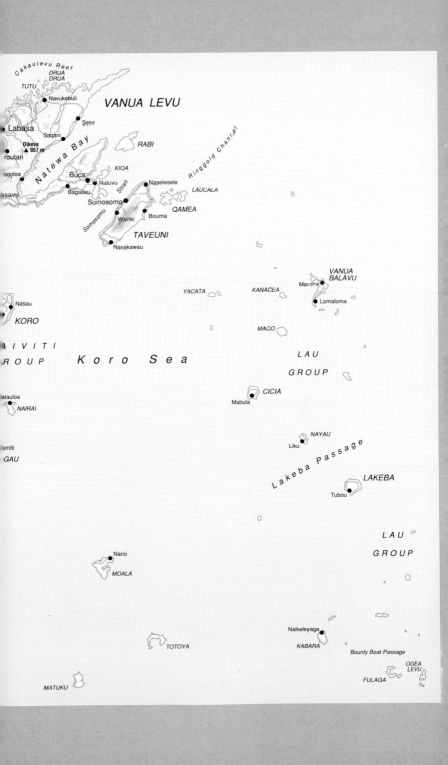

Fiji's 300 islands do not lend themselves to a quick and breezy visit. Many visitors are happy to be disposed by their travel agent to some island resort which offers dazzling white sand beaches beneath coconut palms and a lagoon of pastel greens, turquoises and deep blues. But for intrepid explorers who want to pack in as much as possible within the space of their holiday, Fiji has much to offer, and I have attempted to sign-post what I believe will not only be most enjoyable, but also the best value for money.

The islands of Viti Levu and Vanua Levu comprise more than 80 percent of the total land mass. The International Airport is situated at Nadi on the western side of Viti Levu, the largest island in the Fijian group. The airport is situated on the sunny 'dry' side of the island, within close proximity to the popular Yasawa and Mamanutha islands and the Coral Coast, a term used to describe the resort area from Momi Bay to the Pacific Harbour on Viti Levu.

The Nadi area on Viti Levu is where most of Fiji's resorts are situated and the itineraries assume the visitor will spend at least the first few days here. But you could also choose to stay anywhere else on Viti Levu, or the surrounding islands for that matter, and still use the itineraries I've suggested.

Picture postcard beaches

The three day itineraries – a cruise to the Mamanutha islands and two land tours which span from the east to the southern coast and the westerly capital of Suva – are a wonderful introduction to Fiji as they take in the many diverse attractions of this island. Itinerary *Day 3* gives you the option of spending the night at Suva.

DAY ①

Day Cruise to Mamanutha Islands

There is no finer introduction to Fiji than a cruise from Nadi to the scattered island jewels of the nearby Mamanutha group. This is also a wonderful way to get over jet lag.

Several cruises leave each morning and return late in the afternoon. Buses pick up guests from hotels in the **Nadi** area and from the various resorts on the **Coral Coast** and deposit their eager cargo on the beach, ready for the transfer to a cruise of their choice.

The prices vary but most of the cruises cost between F$50 and F$74 for the day, inclusive of lunch. For those who wish to strike out on their own, it is possible to hire a 'water taxi' for a day of island-hopping at your own pace. The price depends on the craft chosen, but can be as low as F$229 or as high as F$1,200 for the whole day.

For those prepared to pay more than double the going rate and enjoy the company of a limited number of guests, I would recommend a cruise on the schooner-rigged motor yacht, *Whale's Tale*. This is truly a sybaritic experience which begins the moment you board this magnificent 30-m (98½-ft) luxury yacht at

A cruise on board the Whale's Tale

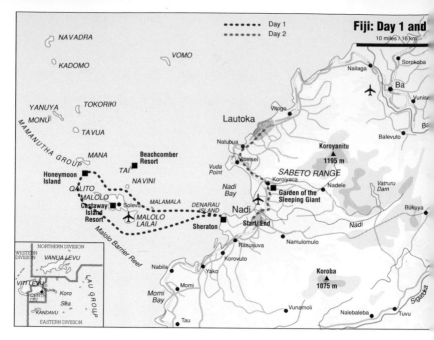

9.45am and find a champagne breakfast awaiting your arrival. The breakfast, a sumptuous meal and all beverages including beer, spirits and wines, and snorkelling gear are included in the price.

The anchor weighed, halyards pulled tight to set the sails, course set for Honeymoon Island, the adventure begins! *Whale's Tale* passes the islands of **Malamala**, **Navini**, **Malolo Lailai** and **Malolo** before reaching its own exclusive destination – **Honeymoon Island**.

There is a magnificent beach and the island is fringed with a colourful coral reef ideal for snorkelling. There is time to explore the island and the reef before lunch is served on board.

The return voyage in the afternoon takes an alternative route around **Castaway Island** and the south-western side of Malolo and Malolo Lailai islands, passing a number of resorts on the way and making an additional stop should time permit.

Whale's Tale returns to its anchorage just before sunset. There is still time for guests to enjoy entertainment and cocktails on the poop deck while viewing the sunset and the torch-lighting ceremony on Denarau Island beach. The rate for adults is F$155 inclusive of pick-up from hotels in the Nadi area.

Check with your hotel tour desk for information on the range of cruises available and confirm the current rates. You can also book a place on the *Whale's Tale* directly at Tel: 722455 or 723590.

There are at least eight other day cruises available from the Nadi-Lautoka area. If the *Whale's Tale* is not available

Aerial view of Malolo Lailai

because it has been fully booked, or because of budget considerations, or if you are already staying on an island resort, there are other cruise options to choose from.

Also operating from Denarau Marina is **Captain Cook Cruises** which operates two vessels: the square-rigged brigantine *Ra Marama*, and the luxury motor vessel, *Duchess of the Isles*. The former offers a similar day cruise, and adventure cruises which include camping on deserted beaches while the latter offers 3-day, 2-night cruises. Book at your hotel travel desk or directly at Tel: 701823, Fax: 710045. Another alternative is **South Sea Cruises** which operates day cruises, half-day cruises, semi-submersible reef-viewing cruises and boat transfers to the various resorts in the Mamanutha Islands. Call South Sea Cruises directly at Tel: 722988/700144, Fax: 720346, or book through your hotel tour desk.

DAY 2

Garden of the Sleeping Giant and Viseisei Village

A leisurely day that starts with a visit to the Garden of the Sleeping Giant with its orchids galore. The Viseisei Village is next where you get a glimpse of Fijian village life. If time permits, a visit to the sugar producing town of Lautoka.

A visit to the **Garden of the Sleeping Giant** (Monday to Saturday 9am–5pm, closed Sunday) will yield something for everyone. For orchid lovers it is pure bliss. For others, it is an experience they seldom forget. Even those who do not care about flowers are struck by the beauty of the gardens when they leave.

The garden occupies 20ha (50 acres) of gently sloping land at the base of the Sabeto Range and takes its name from the silhouette of a giant who appears to be asleep on top of the mountains. Allow a 25-minute drive from the Nadi area towards Lautoka. Drive past the airport and when you have covered 5km (3 miles) you will arrive at the **Wailoko Road** turn-off. Look for a sign on a lamp post on the right-hand side and then turn right into Wailoko Road. Drive another 2km
(1 mile) to the entrance of the garden – a verdant greenscape of bush, trees, ponds and more than 150,000 orchids comprising some 1,200 species, 30 of which are native to Fiji.

A profusion of orchids

For those who do not wish to hire a car and drive, **United Touring Company** (Tel: 722811) will arrange to pick up guests at the various hotels for a half-day tour to the Garden of the Sleeping Giant and Viseisei Village.

The garden has an interesting history. It was started by the American actor Raymond Burr, who had the intention of developing his own collection of orchids. At that time Burr owned Naitauba Island in Lau – one of the prettiest in Fiji. When he decided to move, he sold his island to a religious sect and transferred the orchid garden to a company in which he remains a shareholder. Since then, the garden, destroyed by a number of hurricanes, has had to be replanted anew.

An attractive reception centre in the style of a Fijian *bure* (traditional thatched hut) with a verandah facing the valley has comfortable cane furniture for visitors. Here, you can sit and admire the view, sip on a cool drink of fruit juice which comes with the admission fee, and then either stroll through the gardens yourself or go on an informative guided tour. There are a profusion of orchids everywhere you go: in the reception area and around it, in and outside shade houses, creeping on the sides of moss-covered banks, and even on the trees. Blooms of every shade and size from rich fat hybrids to tiny little natives will assail your senses. A long walk through one shade house leads to a pond of water lilies, a bridge and a rest area and then continues through jungle interplanted with flowering trees and shrubs. There are seats where you can relax and absorb what you have seen.

Allow 10 minutes for your drive from the garden to **Viseisei Village** (open daily 7am–6pm) before continuing to Lautoka. Legends say that the ancestors of today's Fijians first arrived at **Vuda Point** nearby. The fact that the Chief of Viseisei, Ratu Sir Josaia Tavagia, is the Tui Vuda and is one of the two vice-presidents of Fiji suggests the importance of the *matanitu* (state) in Fijian politics. In pre-European times, several parts of Fiji were recognised as *matanitu* – political confederations which owed allegiance to a paramount chief called a *tui*, the title incorporating the name of the area represented. Thus, the Tui Vuda is the head of the former 'state' of Vuda.

Viseisei Village was also once the home of the former late Prime Minister, Dr Timoci

The Tui Vuda (right) of Viseisei Village

Bird's eye view of Viseisei Village

Bavadra, who was deposed in a military coup in 1987. An imposing *bure* was built for Dr Bavadra and is now very popular as a photographic subject.

The village is off the main road and you will know you have arrived because of the road humps on the main highway. These were built to slow down traffic as fatal accidents used to occur here at an alarming rate. The village has been open to the public for more than 20 years so there is no reason to feel you are intruding or disrupting the villagers' daily routine. The villagers will offer to show visitors around the village and it is appropriate to give a small gratuity to your guide before leaving. The merit of the visit is not so much in seeing the village itself but for the opportunity of meeting the local people on their own turf and seeing something of their way of life.

A large Wesleyan church with a memorial commemorating the centenary of the arrival of missionaries in Fiji in 1835 is a point of interest as is the *bure* of the Tui Vuda.

It is now time to return to Nadi for lunch (see *Eating Out*, pages 70–74) and then an afternoon of shopping or relaxing on the beach. Alternatively, continue to **Lautoka** for a curry lunch at **City Takeaways** at 15 Malau Place, or Chinese food at the **Great Wall of China**, 21 Naviti Street.

Lautoka town owes its existence to a large sugar mill (said to be the biggest in the Southern Hemisphere) and a deep water port. It may be of interest to note that Fiji produces some of the world's best sugar. Lautoka is Fiji's second largest city, but it is small by international standards, with a population only 30,000. There is nothing much of interest in Lautoka except for a sugar cane railway that runs through the centre of the town between a line of tall royal palm trees. From here, the gleaming jewels that make up the southern **Yasawa Islands** are clearly visible offshore.

DAY 3

Nadi to Suva

Travel to the charming capital city of Suva via Queen's Road; driving past scenic sugar cane fields, forests of lush Caribbean pine trees and isolated bays, across the township of Sigatoka to the Tongan Fort, the resorts on the Coral Coast, Pacific Harbour and the Orchid Island Cultural Centre.

It is about 197km (122 miles) from Nadi to the capital city, Suva. This journey will require up to 3 hours of driving with stops for photography on the way. Allow an extra half-hour to visit the Orchid Island Cultural Centre just outside Suva. This will time your arrival in Suva for lunch. If you wish to avoid the long drive back, plan to have more stops along the way, arrive in the early evening and spend the night at Suva. The alternative to doing your own thing is to book a guided tour of Suva with **United Touring** (Tel: 722811)

Because of the distance you will be covering and the spectacular

Coral Coast spans from Nadi to S

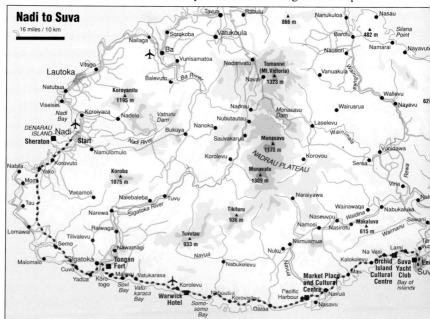

scenery along the way, a self-drive day trip to Suva should begin early in the morning. An 8am start is ideal. The road is well maintained and is tarred all the way. The only hazards are incompetent drivers who overtake at blind corners, or who stop abruptly on the road without pulling to the side; and horses and cattle, which, unrestrained by fences, wander as and where they please. Allow an hour or so to reach the town of **Sigatoka**.

Sigatoka is a pleasant little town on the banks of Fiji's second largest river and benefits from both the farming community and the tourist resorts along the Coral Coast. The site of a former **Tongan Fort** (open daily 8am–5pm) on the southern side of the river at Naroro is worth a visit. To get there, cross the bridge and turn right. It is only 4km (2½ miles) from the turn-off.

About 7km (4¼ miles) past the bridge is the village of **Korotogo**, where the highway joins the **Coral Coast**. From here, the next 35km (21¾ miles) runs beside the lagoon and through a series of villages and resorts. Korotogo marks the southern boundary of the sugar cane growing area. The landscape begins to change as you head towards the south-east. As the prevailing trade winds carry moisture and dump it on this coast the vegetation is lush and the rainforest

View of Korotogo resorts

stretches over hills and mountains as far as the eye can see. There are six places in the Korotogo area – including a big resort hotel and other smaller, more intimate hotels – which offer accommodation and cater for every type of budget and taste.

The next village is **Malevu** with speed bumps to slow traffic down. The road skirts around **Bulu Bay** and then goes around the bigger and more open **Sovi Bay**. The southern side of Sovi Bay is popular with locals. It offers safe swimming away from the crashing surf which at times sweeps into the bay. This is definitely a good spot for a break and a swim – there are parking places by the side of the road – and if you left late rather than early, a picnic lunch after the swim.

Next is the village of **Vatukarasa**. It is laid out in the old Fijian pattern with a handsome chief's *bure* next to the road as you first enter the village, a wide village green with houses and *bures* on each side and a church at the other end. The opening into Vatukarasa Bay is wide and at times allows a big swell to roll in and crash onto the beach. You will pass the resorts of **Tabua**

Sands, the **Hideaway** and **Naviti**, each tucked away among flowers and coconut trees next to its own beach and then reach **Korolevu**, the former site of Fiji's first beach resort. The resort closed some years ago but the property was purchased recently by a new company intent on redeveloping the area into a championship golf course, marina, holiday villas and a five-star resort. At the other end of the bay is the **Warwick of Fiji**, formally the Hyatt Regency.

The stretch of road between **Korotogo** and **Naboutini** is particularly attractive. It winds around bays and climbs low ridges for views of villages and lagoons glimpsed through avenues of coconut palms and rainforest, and then moves away from the coast, climbs a series of low hills and emerges on the coast to briefly join the sea again before reaching the wide expanse of open, flat land at **Pacific Harbour**. The islands of **Yanuca** and **Beqa** are visible offshore.

Pacific Harbour was one of Fiji's most ambitious projects. Several hundred acres of lowland were cleared and drained. Lakes were created and the surrounding land was subdivided and sold. An 18-hole championship golf course designed by Robert Trent Jones Jr and a sumptuous clubhouse was built. A new hotel was constructed beside the beach, probably the longest in Fiji, and a cultural and shopping centre was built around one of the lakes. Investors purchased land, built attractive villas and settled down to a good life which continues to this day. However, the project never realised its potential because the location is prone to a great deal of rain throughout the year and is discouraging to those who want sunshine. It is perfect, however, for those who like gardening.

The **Market Place and Cultural Centre** (open daily 7.30am–6.30pm) built around a waterway, is an ideal place for another break. There

are an assortment of curio shops and restaurants, and regular tours are conducted on the waterway to watch Fijian actors demonstrate ancient rituals.

From Pacific Harbour, the road runs through a widening plain, the monotony broken by huge banyan trees, some of which must take up a quarter acre, with grazing cattle, maize and sorghum plantations, and rice paddies flourishing over the wide expanse of fertile land.

Pacific Harbour

The township of **Navua** is on the eastern bank of the river where land is held in small holdings by Indian farmers who specialise in rice cultivation.

The next point of interest is the **Orchid Island Cultural Centre** (open daily 8am–4.30pm) on the outskirts of Suva. A billboard and a large double-hulled canoe which was built in the Lau Islands and sailed to the city mark the turn-off to the centre. This is one of

Mongoose from Orchid Island

Fiji's most popular attractions and offers something for everyone. A model Fijian village shows the different regional styles of *bure* construction and a replica of the old-style temple, the *bure kalou,* which is so valued that its likeness is used on the Fiji $20 note.

Visitors will be taken on a tour of the chief's *bure* which shows how people lived in pre-European times. On display are weapons, cooking utensils and sleeping arrangements. There are also interesting demonstrations of pottery, basket and mat weaving, and how to make bone fish hooks, fish and crab traps and various other items.

A covered walkway leads the visitor past Fiji's fauna: the rare and unique Fiji banded iguana, birds, mongooses, flying foxes, a harmless snake, turtles and some of the introduced animals, including monkeys – the only ones in Fiji. A pictorial display illustrates myths and legends and aspects of history, including a gruesome chapter on cannibalism. There are also orchids, wild ginger blooms and a walk through rainforest.

About 4km (2½ miles) before you reach the centre of Suva is the **Bay of Islands** and the attractive suburb of **Lami**. The **Tradewinds Hotel** sits on the water's edge; yachts and pleasure craft are moored in the bay in the lee of three islands, and there is a convention centre beside the lagoon. From here, it is 3km (1¾ miles) to the heart of the city, passing through the **Walu Bay** industrial area and the **Royal Suva Yacht Club**.

You can either opt to spend the night at **Suva** and tour the colourful town the following morning (See *Pick & Mix*, page 30), or if you arrive early, tour Suva and then drive back to Nadi. The **Suva Travelodge** (Tel: 301600) along Victoria Parade is a comfortable walk from the city centre and an excellent base It is also a short distance away from major nightclubs and the **Thurston Gardens** and **National Museum**. The **O'Reilley's** complex, which includes three restaurants and two nightclubs, is the most popular with visitors as are the **Golden Dragon** and **Traps** bars found along Victoria Parade.

A bure exhibit at Orchid Island

1. Suva

A half-day tour of the capital city of Suva. Take in the city sights and revel in this melting pot of a dozen different races.

Begin your walking tour at the **Thurston Gardens** (open daily 8am–5pm) and the **Fiji Museum** (Monday to Thursday 8am–4.30pm, Friday 8am-4pm, Saturday 9am–4pm, closed Sunday). Established in 1904, the museum is a gem. It holds the most comprehensive collection of Fijian artefacts in existence as well as a collection from other Pacific islands. A double-hulled canoe that was built at the turn of the century – and used in the making of the movie *His Majesty O'Keefe*, starring Burt Lancaster – commands your attention at the main hall. The Thurston Gardens houses a large and interesting collection of flora from the South Pacific.

Return to **Victoria Parade** and turn left into Queen Elizabeth Drive. This brings you to the gates of the **Government House**, the state residence of the President of Fiji. A guard in red tunic and white *sulu* at the gate is a favourite photographic subject. If you continue beside the sea, you will reach the **University of the South Pacific** campus, built on a former seaplane base. The base played a critical role in the war in the Pacific against invading Japanese by mounting long-range reconnaissance missions and mercy flights which saved many lives.

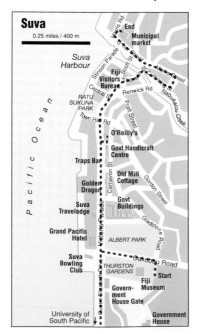

Soldier at the Government House

Retrace your steps up Queen Elizabeth Drive into the main drag of Victoria Parade, past Thurston Gardens and Albert Park on your right, and Suva Bowling Club and the Travelodge on your left. Turn right into Macarthur Street opposite O'Reilly's and allow 2 hours to explore the heart of the city's commercial section. The **Government Handicraft Centre** (Monday to Friday 7am–6pm, Saturday 8am–5pm, closed Sunday) sells a wide range of Fijian handicrafts, including replicas of old weapons, bowls, basketware, and *masi* cloth items, and is well worth a visit.

Retrace your steps to Victoria Parade, turn right and continue to the north. At the end of the block, cross Townhall Road to **Ratu Sukuna Park** on the left. Here, Renwick Road joins Victoria Parade at the triangle with an old *ivi* (native chestnut) tree at its apex and seats at its base. Much of old Suva still survives in Renwick Road. Victoria Parade joins Thomson Street where the old vies with the new, crosses Nabukalou Creek and turns into Cumming Street which in turn joins Renwick Road. Look out for the Fijian women selling handicrafts under the flamboyant tree on the corner of Thomson and Cumming streets. Duty-free dealers also crowd each other here, the oldest unchanged part of Suva.

Stroll up Cumming Street, turn left into Renwick Road and then turn left again into Marks Street which will bring you down to the Thomson Street junction. Continue down towards Usher Street to the **Municipal Market** (open daily 7am–5pm), taking extra care to avoid 'sword sellers' (see *Shopping*, page 69) and 'guides' who will offer to take you to places where you will get the 'best deal'.

The Municipal Market and

Clock tower, Thurston Gardens

adjoining bus-stand cover an entire city block and offer a fascinating glimpse of Fiji's multiracial community. The best days are Friday and Saturday mornings, but the markets may be crowded to the point where it is difficult to walk through. All the products of land, lagoon and ocean are on display here. From the markets, follow **Stinson Parade** along the foreshore, past Ratu Sukuna Park and eventually back to Victoria Parade. Have lunch at one of the restaurants at O'Reilley's, just before the Macarthur Street turning, or at the **Old Mill Cottage** further down at Carnavon Street.

2. Natadola Beach Picnic and Coral Coast Railway

See the historic Momi Bay Guns; a picnic at Natadola Beach, popular with the locals on weekends; ride the toy train Coral Coast Railway; and visit the spectacular Kulukulu sand dunes.

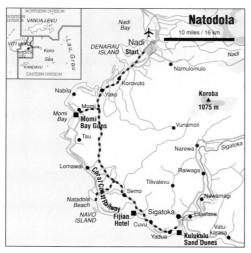

Pack a picnic lunch and drive on the **Queen's Highway** towards Suva. The first point of interest is 15km (9¼ miles) away from town at the Momi Bay turn-off where a sign proclaims a place of historic interest – the site of the **Momi Bay Guns**. These guns are World War II relics restored by the National Trust of Fiji.

Follow the signposts to the location. The guns and the grounds which overlook **Momi Bay** and the main channel in the barrier reef are not spectacular, but may be of interest to those fascinated by the Pacific phase of World War II. The Mamanutha Islands are clearly visible and in fact, this is the closest point to the islands. Return again to the main road and continue south towards Suva.

It takes about 25 minutes to reach the Natadola Beach turn-off at **Maro Road**, 40km (25 miles) from Nadi. Maro Road is signposted and the turn-off is easy to find as there is a mosque on the left, a Hindu temple just above the turn-off on the right, and a sign which says 'Tuva Indian School'. This is still the heart of the sugar cane growing area and the road twists and winds its way to the sea between sugar cane farms and mosques. You cross the river twice and this will confirm that you are on the right road. Keep bearing left. Allow 15 minutes for a comfortable drive from the turn-off before arriving at the beach.

There is more than a mile of magnificent white sand curving in

Picturesque Natadola beach

an arc from Navo Island in the south to the north-west. The prevailing trade winds comes off the land so that the extensive bay is usually calm and ideal for windsurfing. Coral reefs encompass the bay to nearly a mile offshore where a wide passage allows safe entry into the bay. Yachtsmen tend to avoid this anchorage because the wide entrance allows a swell from the south to roll into the bay causing boats to rock uncomfortably. But, the same swell will sometimes produce a low surf ideal for body surfing. The beach is popular with locals who congregate here on weekends picnicking or enjoying barbecues.

Many plans have been put forward to turn the area into a major tourist attraction with resorts, a golf course, marina, shopping centre and condominiums, but fortunately, nothing has quite taken off here and the area remains one of the most attractive pieces of undeveloped real estate. Coral reefs on each side of the bay offer good snorkelling but the main feature is the expanse of white sand.

For a ride of a different kind and a pre-arranged picnic, continue on the main highway for another 15 minutes to the **Coral Coast Railway** (Monday to Saturday, closed Sunday, Tel: 500988) terminal at the Fijian Hotel turn off. From here, the Coral Coast train departs at 10am and reaches Natadola Beach just before noon. It chugs along the track beside the lagoon, through country impossible to enjoy otherwise because there is no other access. A barbecue lunch is served and there is enough time for swimming, snorkelling and horse riding before the departure at 3pm for the 1-hour ride back.

The Coral Coast train ride is great family fun. The railway is part of the network that

All aboard!

was established by the Colonial Sugar Refining Company when it developed the sugar industry. The trains hauled raw sugar cane to Lautoka for processing and when the Fiji government purchased the company in 1970, the railway system was maintained. Today, much of the sugar cane is still hauled to Lautoka on this quaint, narrow gauge railway. An entreprising New Zealander decided to build period coaches, a terminal station at the Fijian Hotel and went into business using the existing infrastructure.

If time permits, continue another 10km (6¼ miles) to the **Kulukulu sand dunes** – one of the most arresting sights in Fiji. The turn-off has a shop and a sign advertising 'Club Masa'. Follow this road to the dunes, park your car and ascend the dunes for panoramic views of the sea, the Sigatoka River where it meets the ocean, and the dunes. The highest point of the sand dunes rises no more than 30½m (100ft) above sea level, but they are spectacular nevertheless.

Some of Fiji's most important archaeological finds were made on these sands. The winds constantly expose pottery shards and sometimes human remains. The oldest human remains to have been found in the Fiji-Polynesian part of the Pacific came from this site. Fresh water from the Sigatoka River has impaired coral growth and as there is no barrier reef, a large surf usually thunders onto the exposed beach. The beach here is the haunt of surfers and windsurfers but only strong swimmers or experienced surfers should venture into the sea here.

3. Nausori Highlands

Hire a four-wheel drive car, prepare a picnic lunch, pack swimming gear and set off to explore something of Fiji's wilderness. Make an early start for a full day of adventure. There are two different routes to choose from, both with equally breathtaking and rugged scenery. Do not attempt both itineraries on the same day.

This is a tour for the experienced driver as the roads can be very treacherous. The car rental company will insist on an indemnity clause as some cars have been damaged through careless or incompetent driving.

A 4-wheel drive is a must

Route 1: Allow 15 minutes from Nadi to the Nausori Highlands road turn-off. The easiest way is to drive south (towards Suva) through the town and turn left at the service station. There is a Hindu temple on the opposite side of the road. Follow this road for 5km (3 miles) and keep your eyes peeled for the **Nausori Highlands** signpost on your right.

From then on there is virtually

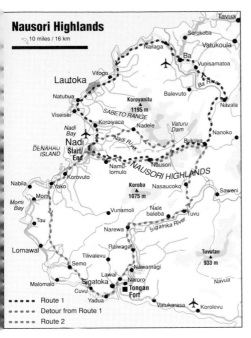

Nausori Highlands

10 miles / 16 km

Tavua
Sorokoba
Nailaga
Vatukoula
Ba
Vunisamatoa
Vitogo
Lautoka
Natubua
Balevuto
Ba River
Viseisei
Koroyanitu
1195 m
SABETO RANGE
Navala
Koroiyaca
Nadele
Vaturu
Dam
Nanoko
Nadi
Bay
Nadi River
Bukuya
DENARAU
ISLAND
Nadi
Start/
End
Namu-
lomulo
Nausori
NAUSORI HIGHLANDS
Korovuto
Nabila
Yako
Koroba
1075 m
Nasaucoko
Saweni
Momi
Mom
Bay
Vunamoli
Nale
baleba
Tuvu
Tau
Narewa
Sigatoka River
Lomawai
Raiwaqa
Tilivalevu
Tuvutau
933 m
Semo
Nawamagi
Lawai
Naroro
Navua
Malomalo
Sigatoka
Cuvu
Tongan
Fort
Vatukarasa
Korolevu
Yadua

•••• Route 1
•••• Detour from Route 1
•••• Route 2

only one road, 34-km (21-miles) long, to the Bukuya turn-off. It leaves the Nadi flats and begins ascending over rolling country of sugar cane farms towards the highlands. The road then turns steeply uphill and follows a narrow ridge with sharp bends.

Massive volcanic rocks and sheer cliff faces overlooking Nadi town, the airport and the offshore islands offer good photographic subjects.

There is a forestry station and village at **Nausori** when you reach the top. Once the site of a sawmill, it is now the centre of an ambitious replanting programme with Caribbean pine. The road leaves the plantations and continues through steep country with rainforest as your company. On the right begins the **Sigatoka River** catchment while to the left is the **Nadi River**. A turn-off to the left marks the access road to **Vaturu Dam**, the source of fresh water for Nadi and Lautoka.

For those who want a less adventurous trip, turn left to the dam and after a picnic lunch, descend via the **Sabeto Valley** to the main highway north of the airport. Otherwise, continue on towards **Bukuya** for another 12km (7½ miles) and turn left before reaching the village. The road now follows the **Ba River** catchment towards

Road between Bukuya and Navala Village

Down the Ba River in a bilibili

the village of **Navala,** 17km (10½ miles) from the junction. On the way there are plenty of picturesque spots to stop for a picnic.

Some time ago, the chief and people of Navala made the decision to keep the village traditional and allow only *bures* to be built for housing. As a result, Navala is a remarkable village and an ideal subject for photography. The village accepts visitors who wish to stay the night. The usual Fijian courtesies should be followed if you intend to visit. This requires the presentation of 1kg (2lb) of *yaqona* (the mildy narcotic powdered root of the piper mysthisticum plant) to the *turaga ni koro* (village headman) with the request that you wish to look around the village and take some photographs.

Allow an hour's careful driving from Navala, 18km (11¼ miles) away, to reach the township of **Ba**. As you descend from Navala, the road passes by sugar cane farms and the compounds of Indian farmers and their families. Some of the fields are perched on ledges, offering testimony to the ingenuity of the farmers. On leaving Navala, the Ba River enters a gorge, the site of Fiji's whitewater rafting. The excitement of the ride depends on the volume of water in the river and for this reason rafting is best after a heavy downpour in the highlands.

The road begins its descent to Ba from a high ridge overlooking the lowlands and the sparkling sea in the distance. Much like the road up to the Nausori Highlands, it is steep and winding until it reaches low ground. The road is tarred some miles before the township and passes by the sugar mill on the banks of the river. The town itself is a quaint one-street collection of shops. Turn left to return to Nadi. You will know you are on the right road when you cross a one-way bridge where traffic is regulated by traffic lights which no one seems to take much notice of. The western side of the river has some rather ostentatious houses built by prosperous Indian merchants. It is now 72km (44¾ miles) from Ba to Nadi and

38km (23½ miles) to Lautoka on a tarred highway. Allow 1¼ hours and an extra 15 minutes during the sugar cane harvest season when you may encounter slow-moving trucks carting cane to the mill. The section between Ba and Lautoka offers great views of sugar cane fields and pine tree plantations on steep hills, and in the distance, Bligh Water and the Yasawa Islands

The distances involved are not great but because of the state of the road, this route, with a stop for a swim and picnic and then a visit to Navala village, will require a whole day.

Route 2: An alternative route, but just as spectacular, is to drive from Nadi onto the Queen's Highway to **Sigatoka** town, 77km (48 miles) away, and from there up the **Sigatoka Valley** road. This will eventually bring you back to Nadi through the Nausori Highlands.

There are many points of interest along this route. The site of a **Tongan Fort** (open daily 8am–5pm) at Naroro seen on the opposite side of the river is worth a visit. This necessitates crossing the Sigatoka River via a one-way bridge and turning left at the end of the bridge. From here, it is 4km (2½ miles) to the village. From its vantage point, the old fort once commanded the Sigatoka River and still offers breathtaking views. Return to the Nadi side of the river and turn right up the valley road to the village of **Lawai** where pottery is still made in the time-honoured Fijian way.

The bountiful fertility of the **Sigatoka River Valley** has earned it the title of the 'salad bowl' of Fiji. A full range of vegetables thrive in the rich soils here, and a government agricultural research station, 6½km (4 miles) from town, is constantly experimenting with new varieties and species. The road up the valley is not tarred and requires attentive driving. It follows the river for most of the way and climbs two steep ridges, offering magnificent scenery. There are villages on the way and 35km (21¾ miles) up the road, tobacco-drying kilns are a distinct landmark at **Nalebaleba**. About 7km (4¼ miles) further, a road on the left leads to Bukuya while the valley road continues to its terminal at Korolevu. Follow the road to Bukuya. There are two villages, both with access roads on the way. The first is **Nasaucoko** village, headquarters of government troops during the Colo war against the mountain people in 1876, two years after the cession of Fiji to Britain. It was here that some of the rebel leaders were hanged and the war brought to an end.

It is 17km (10½ miles) from the time you leave the valley

Navala village, Viti Levu

road and reach the village of **Bukuya**. A little way past the village, take the turn to the left which will eventually you lead back to Nadi. Allow at least 5 hours for each of the two excursions, plus extra time for swimming, picnicking and photography,

Alternatively, book with **Highlands Tours** (Tel: 520285) for a day trip to Nasaucoko village which includes lunch and a visit to the village. Check with your hotel tour desk for more information. The tour covers the same ground as a self-drive excursion up the Sigatoka River Valley, but diverts to Nasaucoko village, where lunch is served, and returns by the same route.

4. Levuka: Fiji's Old Capital

There is no question that the town of Levuka, on the island of Ovalau, off the western coast of Viti Levu is a special place. Time seems to stand still here and those who venture beyond the usual tourist traps will be delightfully surprised with their discovery. This day trip will take in all the major attractions of Levuka, plus an interesting bush walk.

Levuka town, the former Fijian capital, was important for three reasons: the direction of the prevailing east-south-east trade winds which allowed sailing ships to enter and leave port without diffi-

Beach Street in sleepy Levuka

culty; its central position on the island of Ovalau within the Lomaiviti group; and finally, its proximity to the once politically powerful states of Bau, Verata, Rewa and Cakaudrove. When Fiji became a British possession in 1874, Levuka's days as the capital were numbered.

The easiest way to get to Levuka is to fly from Nausori Airport near Suva. The 10-minute flight costs just under F$30 one way. If you're planning to do an island hop, Fiji Air also has a special package which allows you to fly from Nadi to Kadavu, Levuka, Savusavu, Taveuni and return for F$180. As there are four flights to Levuka each day, a morning visit and lunch will accomplish most of the objectives of the casual traveller. Fiji Air, in association with the National Museum offers a special package day tour for just under F$60. The price includes a return flight, morning tea and lunch at Levuka and two optional guided tours: one around the town and the other, a bush walk up the hill. The bush walk ascends to a high point overlooking the town and the adjacent islands. This tour of Levuka is definitely one of the best deals on offer in Fiji.

Levuka town, on Ovalau's south-west coast, sits on a narrow strip of land with a bush-clad mountain directly at its back. It was

Levuka town on the island of Ovalau

the lack of available space which caused the administration to move to Suva and consign Levuka to its memories. It was also this move which caused Levuka to remain in its own time warp. Levuka's main thoroughfare, **Beach Street**, is one of the last unchanged places in the Pacific and various organisations are doing their best to try and preserve it way as a living museum of Fiji's (and the South Pacific's) colourful past.

The fact that Levuka did not decline completely is due to a fish cannery operated by the Pacific Fishing Company which buys skipjack tuna from local and overseas contract fishermen and indirectly pumps money into the local economy. The cannery is located next to the wharf at the southern end of Beach Street, the town's main (and only) thoroughfare. A stroll around the town will take no more than 20 minutes. This will allow a thorough look at most of the town's historic landmarks: the **Catholic Church**, with the cross on the bell tower that also serves as one of the lead-in lights into the harbour; **Levuka Public School** which is the oldest in the country; the **Ovalau Club**; the old **Town Hall** just beside the club; the **Masonic Lodge**; the **Royal Hotel** which is the oldest operating hotel in the Pacific (some parts dating from 1860); and the **Totoga Falls**, reached by following a track from the end of Bath Road.

Approximately 1km (½ mile) south of the cannery is **Nasova** and its commemorative park. This is where Fiji was ceded to Britain in 1874 and where in 1970, Prince Charles on behalf of his mother, Queen Elizabeth II, returned Fiji to the descendants of the chiefs who had given it to Queen Victoria 96 years ago.

The more adventurous should linger a day or so. The **Royal Hotel** (Tel: 440024) has rates which begin at F$14. The **Old Continental Inn** (Tel: 440057) has accommodation from F$7 to F$17 including breakfast. **Mavida Lodge** (Tel: 440051) with rates from F$5 to F$16 per day is one of the best deals in the country. The

Ovalau Resort (Tel: 440329) is the closest you will find to a tourist resort and accommodation consists of restored whaler's cottages on a copra plantation 3km (1¾ miles) north of the town. Rates are from F$20 to F$90. On **Leluvia**, a small outlying island, is the popular, low budget Leluvia Island Resort (Tel: 313366) where the rate for a *bure* and meals is F$20 a day.

5. Ba River Run

Whitewater rafting down the Ba River is an an experience you should not miss. This is a full-day trip and includes lunch.

When the volume of water is high in the **Ba River** because of heavy rainfall (December to April), hurtling through turbulent whitewater in an inflatable raft is an exhilarating experience. When the water is low, however, there is no adrenalin rush. Instead, the raft drifts gently along over limpid waters flanked by majestic bush-covered cliffs. This leisurely tour allows you time to swim and enjoy a picnic lunch surrounded by the raw beauty of Fiji's wilderness.

Aerial view of Ba River Valley

Each morning at 8.30am the **Roaring Thunder Whitewater Rafting Company** (Tel: 780029) picks up would-be rafters in the Nadi-Lautoka area and then heads towards the town of Ba on the road journey to the upper reaches of the Ba River. For those who have not already explored this part of the country (see *Pick & Mix*, page 34), this is an ideal opportunity to enjoy a delightful scenic

Getting tangled on the rocks

drive through sugar cane fields with views of Bligh Water and the Yasawa Islands in the distance.

The road turns south soon after crossing Ba River at the township and runs through the fertile alluvial lowlands before ascending steeply up the highlands. The higher the ascent, the more spectacular the landscape below. The road then turns inland, winding down towards the river with vistas of mountains at every turn and the steep gorge below. The road crosses the Ba River, ascends over the next ridge and while within easy distance of **Navala Village**, arrives at the starting point of the rafting trip.

The company provides an experienced guide who will give you a crash course on the basics of rafting and safety. Also included is lunch, transport to and from the river, and necessary equipment like helmet, life vest and paddle.

6. Navua River Trip

A river journey up the Navua River, followed by a traditional welcome and lunch at Namuamua Village.

The best way to enjoy this tour is to book with **United Touring Company** (Tel: 722811) either directly or through your hotel tour desk. The bus picks up guests from the Nadi hotels from 8am onwards and along the Coral Coast resorts until it arrives at Navua township on the banks of the **Navua River** about 11.30am. A tour guide offers useful commentary along the way.

As **Navua town** is only 20 minutes from Suva, the trip covers most of the Queen's Highway and offers spectacular vistas of sugar cane fields and pine tree forests, with coastal views that delight with the ever-changing colours of the lagoon glimpsed through tall coconut trees.

Navua River and Village Stay
10 miles / 16 km

But the drive, pleasant as it is, is only an appetiser for the main course – the boat ride up the Navua River to Namuamua village. Navua town itself, which serves the farmers of the river delta, is small and rather slow. Many of the quaint buildings are reminiscent of a turn-of-the-century vintage. A market-place spills over onto the footpath and the edge of the road.

Among the many flat-bottom, narrow punts at the jetty are some which come to bring produce to the market every morning and will

Punting up the Navua River

return upriver later in the day. One of these will also take visitors to Namuamua village.

Seated two abreast, hip to hip, the boat will have only a few inches of freeboard. The pilot cranks the outboard engine, the guide sits forward and the voyage begins. About 40 minutes after leaving Navua, the punt will pass by the village of **Nakavu**, the last village with a road access. The river then enters a gorge flanked by bush-clad hills. Look closely and you will see tall tree ferns, vine-clad tree trunks, clumps of bright green, fluffy bamboo and small grassy banks. The river narrows and the punt, like a homing salmon, will find the line of least resistance up frothing rapids. See spectacular waterfalls tumble down cliff faces, some flash like silver behind a screen of bamboo, others majestic as they gush 30m (98½ft) into the river.

It takes an additional 40 minutes to reach Namuamua village, but this can vary, depending on the size of the engine and the amount of water in the river. If the water level is low, it requires manhandling over the shallows, a function performed by the boatmen while the you sit tight. The calm stillness of the river suggests unplumbed depths but often the helmsman just leaps out, tilts the engine up and walks the punt over a shallow bank.

As the punt emerges from the gorge, the country opens up gradually. **Nukusere** village, high on the bank, is the first major settlement easily noticed because of the clutch of colourful river punts moored below. A few hundred metres ahead, on the opposite bank, is the village of **Namuamua**.

School children awaiting your arrival will lead you up into a house where a presentation of *yaqona* is made on your behalf. Once the *yaqona is* served, the guide takes the group on a tour of the village.

A drink of yaqona... followed by lunch

After a hearty lunch of chicken, sausages, dalo leaves in coconut cream and boiled cassava eaten off mats covering the floor, there is a *meke* or communal dance put up by young men. The formal entertainment complete, the band will strike up a tune and invite you to dance. Leaving the village at 3pm, you will arrive at Navua town by 4pm, the trip on the punt downriver taking much less time.

Right: a waterfall seen on
the way up Navua River

EXCURSIONS

7. Namuamua Village Stay

A few days' stay at a village will provide an interesting insight into traditional life, and a chance to experience Fijian hospitality and warmth at its best.

Take the Navua River trip (see *Pick & Mix*, page 41). At the end of the visit inform your hosts that you would like to spend a night or two with them. It does not matter that the villagers have had no prior notification. Just inform your hosts, specifically **Eremasi Tuicaumia** or **Semesa Caginivalu** and they will organise a family who will act as hosts.

If you wish to make an advance booking, a call must be booked with the radio operator in Suva at 311010 to the radio telephone at Namuamua village on the call sign 452 RP2. The village operator will then fetch Eremasi or Semesa.

In making your own arrangements, the following should be the rule: Allow F$30–F$40 for the punt voyage from Navua. F$15 should be allocated for each guest per night for accommodation and food. Additional items such as cans of corned beef, rice, sugar, tea and flour – regarded as luxuries by the villagers – should be purchased in Navua to share with your host family. The quantity depends on the intended length of stay. An additional F$3 should be allowed for a guide for each day that one is required. If you

Preparing yaqona for the welcome ceremony

Villagers and guests at Namuamua

wish to rent horses (there are no saddles) budget about F$5 a day. The guide will be a villager only too happy to show you around, take you hiking, hunting for wild boar or fishing in the river. Take a casting rod as there are large mouth bass to be caught for sport and for your dinner.

Fijian etiquette requires the presentation of *yaqona* (the mildly narcotic root of the piper mysthisticum plant) to your hosts and the whole village will assemble to accept the offering. One kg (2lb) of *yaqona* is more than ample and will cost between F$14–F$18, depending on the market rate. The people of Namuamua cultivate *yaqona* so it is best to purchase it at the village and contribute cash to the village economy.

Many village activities can be experienced without planning. The women can go fishing for prawns and fish; the men can go to plantations or hunt for wild boar. Hiking to nearby villages upstream or to **Nukusere** village downstream requires a guide. There are seven villages upstream. These are **Navuandra**, **Nakavika**, **Navunikambi**, **Saliandrau**, **Naggarawai**, **Wainimakatu** and **Naraiyawa** (see map on page 41). It is possible to make arrangements to stay overnight at these villages also. In the late afternoon there will be a game of touch rugby or volleyball, followed by a bath in the river and a bowl of *yaqona*. In the evenings, villagers and guests will gather to tell stories and play guitars and songs. You will be asked many questions. As Fijians will happily answer any question you ask them, they will expect the same of you.

Navua township is also the port of departure for the island of **Beqa**, about 16km (10 miles) offshore. This is the home of the legendary firewalkers who come from the island, more specifically, from the village of **Rukua** which has now opened its doors to visitors in a low key way. The contact person is **Mikaele Funaki** of Island and Village Tours, GPO Box 14328, Suva, Tel: 340079 or 391002. A 4-day, 3-night visit with a host Fijian family, including all meals, road and boat transport to and from the island will cost you about F$100. A longer stay is also possible.

Beqa Island has renowned coral reefs ideal for swimming and snorkelling. It is a wonderful island for hiking and exploring and for getting to know Fijian people on their own turf.

Firewalkers from Rukua

No stay in Fiji is quite complete without a stay at one of its many island resorts. Beachcomber Resort in the Mamanutha island group caters for varied tastes.

The great Viti Levu barrier reef sweeps in an arc to the north from Momi to the Yasawa Islands and then continues to the north-western extremity of Vanua Levu at Udu Point. Lying in calm water behind the reef near Momi and within close proximity to the Nadi International Airport on Viti Levu are more than two dozen islands that belong to the **Mamanutha** group. These paradisiacal isles have long been acknowledged as among the most beautiful in the world and are now the home of 12 island resorts.

One of the first islands to be developed was **Beachcomber Island**. It was formerly the playground of Fiji-born rancher and butcher Dan Costello. It was his idea of fun to get a boatload of friends on a Friday night, provision adequately with good food and beverages and head for the island to enjoy a weekend of fishing, diving, barbecues and evenings of playing guitars and songs around a campfire.

Sun-drenched beaches When the jet age roared into Nadi in the early 1960s, fun-loving flight crews somehow managed to get included.

The inevitable soon happened: Dan Costello took a lease on Beachcomber island, fitted out an old island trader, named it *Ratu Bulumakau* (Chief Bull) and started daily trips to the island for his guests. The 1-hour trip included entertainment in the form of a string band and a great deal of good clean fun. Pretty soon people said: why don't you build a few *bures* so we can stay longer? That's exactly what Costello did and the **Beachcomber Island Resort** was thus born.

Beachcomber Island is unique among the 12 resorts in the Mamanutha Islands in that it caters to varied tastes, from backpackers who can enjoy accommodation in native-style long house dormitories and all meals for an inclusive price, to the young at heart who can join in the many activities and retire to the privacy of a secluded *bure* where prices are considerably more.

These days, the schooner-rigged *Tui*

Windsurf on transparent waters

Tai sails each day from Lautoka to the island, with connecting courtesy coaches to and from Nadi in the morning and the afternoon, bringing guests and day-trippers who come to enjoy the special ambience the island offers as well as activities such as windsurfing, hobie cat sailing, snorkelling, scuba diving, fishing and parasailing. At night there are entertaining shows and dancing barefoot on the sand.

The reputation established by Costello is jealously guarded by him to this day and the routine of so many years ago is still maintained religiously. Each Friday, Costello boards the *Tui Tai* for the island and spends the weekend there to make sure his guests enjoy themselves as countless thousands of others have done so before them. For more information and bookings call the Lautoka office at Tel: 661500 or Fax: 664496.

Idyllic Beachcomber Island Resort

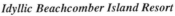

9. Yasawa Islands: The Blue Lagoon Cruise

The Yasawa Islands, lying like a chain of blue beads in the horizon, are reminiscent of the quintessential South Pacific. The Blue Lagoon cruise presents highlights of these islands.

The words, 'blue lagoon' are almost a cliche after two Hollywood movies of the same name showed the world a fantasy of two shipwrecked children cast ashore on a tropical island. Surrounded by nature, they grow to adulthood, find love and happiness and are eventually rescued.

Both movies were shot in Fiji in the **Yasawa Islands**, a group of spectacularly beautiful islands 40km (25 miles) north-west of Lautoka. The first movie, starring Jean Simmons, was filmed in 1948 and the second, less successful remake in 1979 featured Brooke Shields.

A New Zealand naval officer, the late Trever Withers, helped in the original 1948 production. He had come to Fiji with the famed aviator Harold Gatty to see if there were sufficient tuna in Fijian waters for a major fishery. They spent 4 years conducting surveys and reluctantly agreed that there was not enough fish, though time was to prove them wrong as Fiji now has a major cannery.

Withers fell in love with the Yasawa Islands and their people and decided to set up the **Blue Lagoon Cruise**, borrowing the name from the movie. It seemed like a good idea at the time, but he never saw it succeed. After more than 15 years of hard struggle, Withers became ill and sold his interest. Over the

Blue Lagoon Cruise

10 miles / 16 km

Map labels:
GROUP
YEWINI
Muanakuasi Point
Yasawairara
YASAWA
Teci
Saunimolilevu Point
Navotua
Nacula
NACULA
TAVEWA
Sisili
Matacawalevu
NANUYA LAILAI
MATACAWA LEVU
NANUYA LEVU
YAQETA
Matayalevu
Katasomu Point
NAVITI
Somosomo
Soso
Talana Point
NAUKACUVU
NANUYA BALAVU
Wayalevu
WAYA
WAYA LAILAI
Namara
KUATA
YASAWA
VOMO
TOKORIKI
Vitogo
TAVUA
Lautoka
Natubua
TAI
MANA
Viseisei
NAVINI
Koroiyaca
QALITO
Nadi Bay
MALOLO
Solevu
DENARAU ISLAND
Nadi
MALOLO LAILAI
Namulomulo
MAMANUCA GROUP
Korovuto
Nabila
Yako
Momi
Momi Bay
Vunamoli
Tau

Jean Simmons, in the original 'Blue Lagoon'

past 25 years the company has developed an unsurpassed reputation and is considered to be one of Fiji's leading cruise operators and the only one to cruise in the waters around the Yasawas.

It took that amount of time for the rest of the world to discover the islands and people that Captain Withers had found.

The Blue Lagoon trip gives you the full no-holds-barred tropical cruise experience: bright sunny days spent cruising on calm, warm waters, day trips to exotic islands, villages and beaches, dancing barefoot on the sand at night, feasting on food cooked in underground *lovos* and experiencing glorious sunsets with a long cool drink in hand.

Cruise vessels depart virtually every day from the port of Lautoka and offer three different cruises: the original 4-day Blue Lagoon Cruise, a Club Cruise of the same duration and a 7-day cruise. The charm of the Blue Lagoon cruises is the fact that the Yasawa Is-

Crystal clear waters and seafood aplenty in the Yasawas

Coral reefs in the lagoon at Naviti Island, Yasawas

lands are only a short distance from Lautoka – the closest is **Waya** only 48km (30 miles) away – and there is never the feeling of being exposed to the weather in the open sea.

The vessels run through the colourful coral reefs of the Bligh Water to the Yasawa Islands. There are a total of 60 islands stretching in line for more than 80km (49¾ miles), most of which are minuscule except for 10 major ones. The islands are completely undeveloped save for one. The cruise boats weave a magical course between the islands, cruising an average of 4 hours each day to new destinations, usually early in the morning or late in the afternoon so that there is ample time for guests to spend onshore.

Fijian entertainment

The cruise vessels are manned by a Fijian crew, many of whom come from the Yasawa Islands. They are perfect hosts; easy and friendly without being obsequious or patronising. The Fijians generally regard visitors as honoured guests and take pleasure in caring for them. Accommodation is offered in two- or three-bedroom air-conditioned cabins each with an attached bathroom and toilet. Deck cabins have windows while lower cabins have port-holes.

The cruise price includes five meals a day: breakfast, lunch and dinner, and morning and afternoon tea with freshly baked cakes and pastries. The menu is varied, with Fijian, Indian and European dishes, complemented by lavish buffets, outdoor beach barbecues of unlimited steaks, salads and fruits, and island theme nights where the food is cooked in underground *lovos* and accompanied by traditional Fijian entertainment.

Fares start from F$720 for sharing a B deck triple cabin to F$1,661 for single occupancy in an A deck cabin on the 4-day Blue Lagoon Cruise. The 7-day cruise is priced between F$1,309 and F$3,113 for the same type of accommodations. The 4-day Club cruise which offers berths on the new Princess-class boats and other luxurious perks, costs approximately F$200 more for each category of cabin chosen.

Bookings can be made at Tel: 661622/661268, Fax: 664098, or through your travel agent.

10. Viti Levu: Interior Hike

There are ample rewards awaiting the adventurer bold enough to leave his air-conditioned room and venture into the rugged interior of Fiji. You have the option of either booking a trek with a local agent who will make all the arrangements, or follow the recommended 4-day itinerary I have devised.

In 1970 I took a 5-day hike through the interior of **Viti Levu**. My guide at that time was 60-year-old **Ilai Naibose**. We became good friends. I paid his fee and gave him a donation and plenty of advice on how to start his own business. Thus, **Inland Safaris** was born. Naibose is now 82 years of age, but his legs are still strong and on occasions he happily disappears into the bush with a tour party and shows them the 'real' Fiji and the 'real' Fijians.

I have been back in the interior of Viti Levu several times but the memory of that first trip with Naibose is as vivid today as it was when we finished our hike. From Tavua town, we travelled a zigzag road in an old bus up the face of Fiji's highest mountain range to the forestry settlement at Nadarivatu and spent the first cool night at an elevation of more than 607m (2,000ft) above sea level. The next day, we followed an ancient trail on mountain ridges, through rainforest and across sparkling mountain streams to Navai, and then onto Nadrau, almost in the very heart of the main island. Early the next morning, we set off on the longest hike of the trip –

Friendly villagers you will meet on your hike

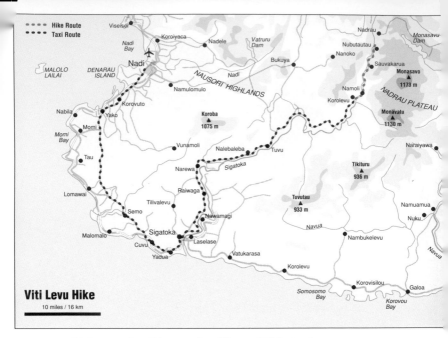

Viti Levu Hike

10 miles / 16 km

10 hours of walking to the village of **Nubutautau**.

It was always my ambition to see this village because it is famous in Fiji's history as the place where the missionary Reverend Baker was killed and eaten in 1867 – a time when most other parts of Fiji had accepted Christianity and given up cannibalism. Our first view of the village was through forest giants on a high ridge above the valley.

It was a peaceful settlement of a few *bures*, the village having been moved from a naturally strong position to open ground. We arrived late in the afternoon, in time to be welcomed by the great, great grandchildren of the chief who ordered Baker killed and were even shown the axe with which the blow was struck.

Many stories have been offered for Baker's death – the only missionary ever killed by Fijians – and even Jack London wrote of the event, citing Baker's ignorance of Fijian etiquette as the reason he was killed. According to one story, Baker had a comb which he used in the presence

Interior, Viti Levu

of the chief. By all accounts it was a handsome comb of whalebone and the chief asked to see it, placing it in his hair and thus laying claim to it in the old Fijian custom. Baker, seeing that it was not returned, rose, walked to the chief and took it out of his hair, committing in Fijian eyes the greatest profanity of all as a chief's head is always held sacred by his people. Baker's fate was sealed.

The most likely cause of Baker's death, however, was political. A whale's tooth (*tabua*) was sent up to Nubutautau by a faction opposed to Christianity. The chief accepted the *tabua* and ordered Baker killed.

I was taken to the exact spot where Baker fell. A small mound of stones in the shade of tall bamboo was the only memorial of this event. Since then, an act of atonement was performed by the villagers and a small memorial erected. Three days later, we emerged at the Keyasi in the Sigatoka River valley and took a bus back to the coast.

The original stonewash

Ilai Naibose and Inland Safaris will show you this world or at least a small part of it, depending on how much time you have. Naibose can be contacted through the Fiji Visitors Bureau or at Tel: 361940. He does not go to Nubutautau now as the trip is too demanding for most people, but on request he will take you there.

The main route Ilai uses now is via a feeder road from the **Yaqara** cattle station on the north-west side of Viti Levu to **Nananu** village from where a trail leads over the **Nakauvadra Range** to the head waters of the **Wainibuka River**. Naibose will arrange a trip from 3 to 10 days which will also include a boat trip to the island of **Moturiki**. The accommodation, road and sea transportation, and food are provided by host families in the villages and the cost per day is about F$60 a person.

If you are sufficiently fascinated by the stories behind the village of Nubutautau and Naibose cannot take you there, I've devised a special hike for those who would like to do their own thing. Make sure you are adequately prepared with extra clothes, mosquito nets, insect repellent and a small medical kit, flashlight, food such as corned beef, sugar, tea, rice and flour packed to be watertight, and packets of cigarettes and money in small denominations. If you like fishing, take a casting rod and lures with you as the rivers are full of bass. A taxi from Nadi up the Sigatoka Valley to Korolevu Village at the end of the road will cost approximately F$100 one way. Stop on the way at Sigatoka to purchase your necessary supplies.

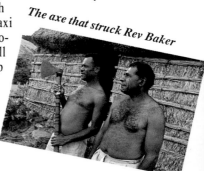

The axe that struck Rev Baker

If you want to enjoy local flavour and lower cost, 3-ton trucks, equipped with seats depart Sigatoka for Korolevu between 2pm and 4pm each day except Sunday. Buy 1kg (2lb) of lamb chops and fresh bread for the first night; cheese for sandwiches for lunch the following day and 500g (1lb) of *yaqona* (the mildly narcotic root of the piper mythisticum plant) for your *sevusevu* (presentation to the chief). Thereafter you can purchase *yaqona* in each village when you first arrive. Divide your purchases into daily rations so you can give your host family two cans of corned beef, 1kg (2lb) of flour, rice and sugar, and a packet of tea and sweets for the children. Double the ration if there are two of you. The men will greatly appreciate a packet of cigarettes.

The car journey will take more than 3 hours if you stop to take pictures as you ascend up the valley road. Try and arrive before 2pm so there is plenty of time to make arrangements to spend the night in the village. On arrival at **Korolevu village** ask to see the

Fishing, Viti Levu

Turaga ni Koro, the village administrator. Explain that you want to spend the night and then go with him to present your *sevusevu* to the chief. Also explain that you wish to spend a few days up the river on your way to Nubutautau and arrange for someone to go ahead to prepare accommodation at the villages of **Sauvakarua** and **Nubutautau**. Make sure you arrange for a horse to carry your baggage and supplies.

Everything is now set for a most enjoyable time. Though I have done these hikes many times, I still enjoy the evening baths in the river, the fishing and hunting, the huge, tasty meals which in retrospect seem like feasts, and above all, the quiet, measured pace of village life and the open, friendly faces of the people.

As you leave the next day, give your host family F$15 to F$20 for each guest in your group. Allow F$3 per day for your guide and F$5 for the horse. The guide will be a villager who will be only too happy to take you to the next village. Your host family or the Turaga ni Koro will make all the necessary arrangements. Make sure you confirm the fee first. A hard day's trek will take you past the village of **Namoli** to your first destination, **Sauvakarua**.

The next day's march is shorter and brings you to the infamous **Nubutautau,** site of the Rev Baker's misfortune. For those who have time, spend 2 days in each village. An overnight at the villages of Korolevu, Sauvakarua and Nubutautau, and back to Sauvakarua and return to Korolevu will take 4 days. Return to Sigatoka on the village truck.

Sauvakarua Village

Savusavu harbour and township

11. Exploring Fiji's North

For those who venture off the beaten track, the north of Fiji offers wonderful rewards. Allow at least a week for a general tour, with stays at resorts and islands along the way. There is no fixed itinerary, instead I've given general directions and recommendations on where to stay. Tailor your exploration of this area according to the time you have. Those seeking some of the best scuba diving in the world should plan to make this area their destination for the duration of their holiday.

The 'north' is a general term applied to the islands of Vanua Levu, Taveuni, Qamea, Laucala, Rabi, Kioa, Matagi and the magical Ringold Isles, as well as Heemskirk Reef, Qelelevu, Wailangilala and Duff Reef. The largest of these islands is **Vanua Levu**, comprising 5,535sq km (2,137sq miles) and second only to Viti Levu which is nearly double in size. Vanua Levu is irregular in shape, running on a south-west to north-east axis for approximately 161km (100 miles) and seldom exceeding 48km (30 miles) in width.

As in Viti Levu, there is a mountainous interior which runs the length of the island and is closer to the east coast, where it traps the moisture-laden south-east trade winds and divides the island climatically. The east tends to have

Yacht regatta, Savusavu

much more rain than the west. Sugar cane is grown on the western side and Labasa, which grew up around the sugar mill, rivals Lautoka as Fiji's second largest city after Suva.

The easiest way to get to Vanua Levu is to fly to **Savusavu** either from Nadi or Suva. Sunflower Airlines flies from Nadi and Fiji Air operates from Suva daily (*Practical Information*, page 85). Savusavu is on the eastern coast of Vanua Levu, occupying a strategic position in the middle of the island. The township nestles around one of the most beautiful natural harbours in the Pacific and is a major port of entry to Fiji.

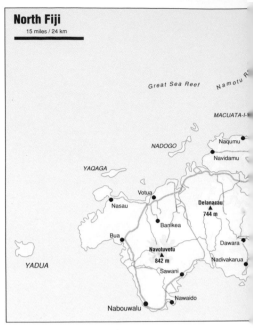

North Fiji

15 miles / 24 km

Great Sea Reef

Namotu R.

MACUATA-I-

NADOGO

Naqumu

Navidamu

YAQAGA

Votua

Nasau

Delanacau
744 m

Banikea

Bua

Navotuvotu
842 m

Dawara

Nadivakarua

YADUA

Sawani

Nawaido

Nabouwalu

The commercial centre of Savusavu hugs a narrow coastal strip beside the harbour. **Nawi Island** is immediately offshore and the deep water between the island and the town is a perfect anchorage for visiting yachts. The road follows the bay towards **Lesiaceva Point** and there are a number of hotels and resorts on this stretch. The **Na Koro** resort features a reception and dining area in the style of a *bure kalou* (ancient temple) and accommodation *bures* tucked among coconut trees and flowering bougainvillea.

The main road runs north-east over the hill and along the coast, passing **Namale Plantation Resort** and soon after, the **Kon Tiki Resort** (Tel: 850262) which is probably the most interesting in Vanua Levu. The resort was originally built by a local nature-lover

Bure-style Na Roro Resort

who turned the 61ha (150 acres) of the old copra plantation into a perfect hideaway from the busy world. There are interesting walks through its own rainforest where 22 of Fiji's 45 native birds may be observed.

There is a stream with waterfalls to splash around in and a nine-hole golf course, two tennis courts, volleyball court, and for those who cannot unplug completely, a satellite TV link. The resort has a wide frontage to the lagoon and its own small boat harbour with direct access through the barrier reef to the sea which offers both excellent scuba diving and deep sea fishing. Accommodation rates begin at F$25 and go up to F$200 per day.

56

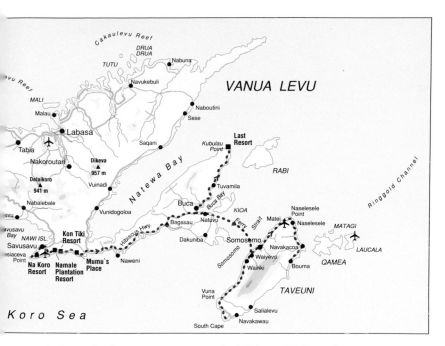

As it was in the past, so too now, the **Hibiscus Highway** between Savusavu and Buca Bay attracts interesting people seeking an alternative lifestyle. For some reason, North Americans in particular seem drawn to this part of Fiji. A short distance along the road from the Kon Tiki Resort, retired US Air Force Colonel Gordon Edris has a small hotel called **Mumu's Place**, open to visitors seeking budget accommodation.

It is 60km (37¼ miles) from Savusavu to Buca Bay along this scenic highway, while another road turns left 3km (1¾ miles) past the Kon Tiki to join **Natewa Bay**, continuing for 130km (81 miles) in a grand sweep around the bay, crossing the mountains and eventually reaching **Labasa**, the largest town in Vanua Levu.

The main road continues on past the Natuvu turn off (the ferry point to Taveuni) to its terminal at Napuka, passing **Tuvamila** estate owned by Laurie Simpson, son of a local self-made millionaire David Simpson and his wife Dorothy. Laurie, who is in his eighties, still runs the plantation. Accommodation is available nearby at **Natuvu Plantation** which is also the terminal for the ferry service to Kioa Island and Taveuni. The plantation is owned by an American company and features a choice of accommodation from dormitories to rooms and *bures*. Guests have access to its many activities, including mountain and jungle hikes, fishing, snorkelling and river rafting in a *bilibili*.

Further along, a group of alternative lifestyle Americans purchased a property at **Kubulau**, just before the end of the road, and called it the **Last Resort**. Sadly, it never achieved its ambi-

The Simpsons of Tuvamila

The abandoned Last Resort

tion as a budget guest house and is now minded by a caretaker.

Two islands offshore, **Rabi** and **Kioa**, are home to different communities. Rabi was purchased for the people of Banaba (Ocean Island) whose home was mined for phosphate. Royalties from the sale of phosphate paid for this island, while the smaller Kioa Island was purchased on behalf of the people of Tuvalu, who were given the island in recognition of their work with the US armed forces in the war against Japan.

A daily bus service from Savusavu departs at 10am and reaches Natuvu at 1pm, in time to connect with a small ferry for the 2-hour trip to **Waiyevo** on the island of Taveuni. It is a scenic drive with local flavour and to me offers more than a brief plane hop to Taveuni or the ferry trip from Savusavu to Taveuni. If you plan to do just Taveuni and skip Vanua Levu, there is a direct flight from Suva and another one via Savusavu from Nadi.

The ferry from Natuvu often stops at Kioa on its way to Taveuni and then continues to the settlement of Waiyevo at about the middle of the island on the north-west coast. Taveuni is Fiji's third largest island and geologically, its most recent. It is of volcanic origin and is known as the 'garden isle' because of its rich soils and luxuriant vegetation which includes large tracts of rainforest and a profusion of bird life.

The 180th meridian of longitude passes through the island of Taveuni at a point slightly to the west of Waiyevo, and in theory, it is possible to straddle this line where it passes through the road so that one foot will be in the 'today' zone and the other in 'yesterday'. However, for purposes of keeping Fiji in the same time zone, this distinction is often ignored.

A copra plantation

Soon after crossing the dateline, you reach the settlement of **Wairiki**, dominated by a large Catholic church and a cross on the hill above it. The spot marks the scene of a crucial battle where the hitherto undefeated forces of the Tongan chief Ma'afu suffered a decisive loss against the locals led by the Tui Cakau.

The climate and fertility of Taveuni attracted European planters and to this day, some of the estates are owned by their descendants. The Soqulu estate, 3km (1¾ miles) south of Wairiki, was part of an ambitious subdivision in the 1970s by an American. The large copra

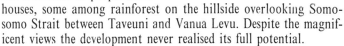

Spear dance, Somosomo Village

plantation was turned into a community with a club house, tennis courts, a small but fascinating golf course and a series of tarred roads from the sea shore up to the mist shrouded mountains.

Blocks of land were sold and a number of people built houses, some among rainforest on the hillside overlooking Somosomo Strait between Taveuni and Vanua Levu. Despite the magnificent views the development never realised its full potential.

It is 20km (12½ miles) from Waiyevo to **Vuna** at the southern end and an additional 7km (4¼ miles) to **South Cape**. The drive north-east from Waiyevo is equally spectacular. The road passes the settlement and village of **Somosomo**, seat of the Tui Cakau (Lord of the Reef), paramount chief of the province of Cakaudrove. The current incumbent, Ratu Sir Penaia Ganilau, is also the President of Fiji. It continues along the coast to **Naselesele Point** and the airport at **Matei**, and then bears to the south-east to reveal a colourful lagoon dotted with small islands and the bigger islands of Qamea and Laucala. There are a number of places offering accommodation near the airport.

Navakacoa landing, 8km (5 miles) from the airport, is the pick-up point for the islands of Qamea, Laucala and Matagi. Each island has a resort hotel. **Laucala** was purchased by publishing tycoon, the late Malcolm Forbes, who turned it into a private playground and willed his remains to be interred on the island. The island has a small, exclusive resort with prices to match.

Probably the most attractive resort in the north of Fiji is on **Matagi Island** (Tel: 880260), a 97-ha (240-acre) copra plantation

Matagi Island with Horse Shoe Bay

operated by the Douglas family. The island lies 10km (6¼ miles) from **Navakacoa** landing, and the resort with its distinct *bures* built on a hexagonal plan is located beside a beautiful white sand beach facing **Qamea Island** with a blue lagoon between. The family-run resort is limited to 24 guests at any one time and operates two live-aboard dive vessels, taking full advantage of some of the most superb diving and cruising in the world. The opposite side of the island has the famous **Horse Shoe Bay** and beach. There is a full programme of activities, including village tours and an excursion to the **Bouma** waterfalls on mainland Taveuni.

It is some 7km (4¼ miles) from Navakacoa landing to the Bouma waterfalls. There is a nominal admission fee and a 5-minute walk to the waterfalls which is one of the most spectacular in Fiji. A large volume of water gushes from a height of more than 22m (70ft) down into a pool surrounded by lush rainforest. A cool, refreshing swim and picnic (barbecue facilities available on site) are highly recommended.

12. Toberua Island Resort

A number of small and super exclusive resorts in Fiji, some with private beaches to frolic on and prices to match, guarantee a sinfully self-indulgent experience.

Fiji's 300 islands offer something for everyone, and resorts have been built to cater for varying tastes and budgets, from those of multi-millionaires to backpackers. **Toberua Island**, tucked away among a maze of coral reefs in Fiji's Bau Waters between the mainland of Viti Levu and the island of Ovalau, and several others such as **Wakaya**, **Vatulele**, **Turtle Island** and **Kaimbu** resorts are in a category and class apart.

Reef golf at Toberua at low tide

Each of these island resorts cater to a small number of guests and then pampers and spoils them non-stop. Some, like Kaimbu Island in northern Lau, are so exclusive that there are only three luxurious guest cottages, each with its own private beach, and a rate of almost US$1000 a day for two people.

Toberua Island Resort is a gem. This tiny island of 1.6ha (4 acres) is a miniature botanic garden with 14 guest *bures* built by Fijian craftsmen in a style that honours their highest chiefs.

Toberua Island Resort was one of the first in Fiji to see the need for a small exclusive island resort and set about creating the conditions and ambience which would appeal to the discerning up-mar-

A beach to call your own

ket traveller. Toberua does not only provide luxurious accommodation and superior cuisine – many places in the world can do this – but has succeeded in creating an atmosphere where the unique nature of the island, the Fijian staff and the culture of the people in nearby villages has melded into harmonious style. Guests begin their adventure from the **Nakelo** landing beside an old trading post on the **Navualoa River,** in the heart of the Rewa River delta, which lies a few minutes from the Nausori International Airport. The 40-minute boat ride down the river is a most appropriate way to begin the holiday.

The island is within sight of some of Fiji's most historic landmarks. To the north-west is the island of **Bau**, the seat of Fiji's highest chiefs; to the south-west the **Kaba Peninsula** where Fiji's last great battle was fought; to the north-east, the island of **Ovalau** and the old capital, **Levuka**.

The daily programme includes many options – even playing golf on the reef at low tide! Besides the usual assortment of watersports like paddle boards, hobic cats and windsurfers, there are fishing trips and scuba diving excursions for certified divers, and of course, snorkelling. For nature lovers, there are boat trips to nearby villages and to uninhabited sand keys and bird sanctuary islands as well as picnics at these romantic locations.

Toberua Island Resort can be reached directly at Tel: 479177, Fax: 302215, or through the Suva office, Tel: 302356. There is a high price to pay for such exclusivity though. Reckon on spending at least F$550 a day on accommodation, food and beverages, and transfers to and from the island.

Toberua Island lies among a maze of reefs in the Bau Waters

Activities

13. Scuba Diving

For many years it was a well-kept secret that Fiji had something special to offer the dedicated scuba diver. The secret is out now and

One of many dive sites in Fiji

even though there are more than 30 dive operators who offer their services, including certification training, there are so many islands and the reef complex is so vast that only a minuscule part of it is regularly seen by visiting divers.

This may change one day, but never to the point that dive locations become too crowded. One of the most attractive aspects of scuba diving in Fiji is the great variety of marine life the waters surrounding the islands offer. The names of some of the famous dive sites suggest their diversity: The Blue Ribbon Eel Reef, The Ledge, Fish Factory Corner, Cabbage Patch, Korolevu, Jack's Place, Yellow Tunnel, Barracuda Hole, Small White Wall, Annie's Bommie and The Zoo. The bonus is that all these sites are found in the same area!

There are amazing underwater experiences to be had: take as an example, The Great White Wall of Taveuni, where you enter a tunnel at the top of the reef at a depth of 9m (30ft) and exit at 27½m (90ft) on the face of a vertical wall covered with a lush, profuse growth of soft white coral as far as the eye can see. Patrolling the face of the wall is an abundance of multi-coloured fish, so tame that they brush fearlessly against you. Next, you ascend to 17m (55ft) and enter another tunnel which takes you to the top of the reef at 11m (35ft).

As Bill Gleason writes in *Skin Diver* magazine: 'When every island claims to be the ultimate travel adventure, the extraordinary disappears and what is described as the 'ultimate' becomes common. Welcome to the islands of Fiji where the extraordinary still exists. For here, the knowledgeable and discriminating diver can find superb world class diving, a different and friendly culture and a variety of accommodation....'

It is significant that for 3 years in a row – 1990, 1991 and 1992 – the Cousteau Society has chosen Fiji as the 'Pacific Ocean Search' expedition venue for its members. This is a wonderful testimonial not only to the superb diving to be found, but also to Fiji as a tourist destination.

There are now a number of small resorts catering almost exclusively for divers. These offer a range of diving courses and trips with full equipment for rental and are invariably located near the best dive sites. Some of these sites are **Beqa Island**, **Kadavu Island** and **Astrolabe Lagoon**, **Wakaya Island**, **Savusavu Barrier Reef**, **Namenalala Island**, and **Taveuni**, **Matagi**, **Qamea** and **Laucala** islands. What can you expect to find? A profusion of tropical hard and soft corals and fish – including sharks – in a bewildering kaleidoscope of colours and shapes. Look out also for a stunning variety of caves, overhangs, walls and drop offs.

An itinerary can be arranged to dive at a number of different locations or on a live-aboard dive boat. Rather than recommend any particular diving spot or boat, I suggest that the serious diver with no knowledge of Fiji get in touch with **Sea Fiji Limited** (P.O. Box 264, Savusavu) at Tel: 850345, Fax: 850344. This company, which specialises in diving holidays, will custom-fit an itinerary based on a questionnaire filled out by the interested party. Sea Fiji will arrange everything, including air transportation.

Colourful reefs and clear waters make Fiji a top dive spot

14. Fishing

Fishing in Fiji can be divided into a number of categories and appeals to different tastes. There is deep sea game or sport fishing for such renowned game fish as marlin, sailfish, yellowfin, dog-tooth

tuna, shark, wahoo, giant trevally and mahimahi (dolphin fish). There is also fishing for ground fish which the whole family can enjoy in the shelter of the lagoon, and there is fishing from the shore, where the true angler casts his lure among patches of coral to hook such varieties as the powerful tropical trevallys, barracuda, queenfish, coral trout and the Spanish mackerel. Finally, there is

Lobsters for the picking

the art of fly fishing for the wily bonefish on tidal flats.

Apart from fishing in the sea, Fiji's rivers also thrive with freshwater varieties waiting to be hooked. The rivers are home to large mouth bass and it is possible to drive to remote and beautiful places for a day's fishing, or to make arrangements to hire a punt or an inflatable raft to drift downstream while casting for fish.

Most resort hotels include game fishing as part of the optional activities available to guests. Some of the resorts own and operate their own fishing boats; others operate boats in association with sub-contracting companies.

How good is fishing in Fiji? As good as, if not better than in Hawaii, says Max Lane of the **Ocean Pacific Club** (Tel: 304864) near Suva, whose resort is the only one in Fiji that caters to game fishing enthusiasts and specialises in looking after fishermen. Lane also runs the only live-aboard fishing boat, the *Adi Kuila,* and on a recent 5-day trip on the boat caught and released one marlin and had five others strike the lure.

Unlike Hawaii or New Zealand where there are scores of game fishing boats roaming the seas, Fiji's waters are relatively unexploited. Most of the areas where grand billfish would be expected to run are seldom fished at all.

Prices for a day's deep sea game fishing in Fiji will depend on the type of boat you decide to hire but can cost more than F$1,000 a day. Smaller boats will cost F$500 and up. The Ocean Pacific Club's *Adi Kuila*, which accommodates up to six people comfortably, costs F$1,200 per day including all meals and tackle, and F$860 for a full day's charter. Those who would like to know how to get the best out of fishing in Fiji should contact Max Lane at Tel: 303252, Fax: 361577.

Right: grinning with their catch

64

Shopping

Shopping in Fiji falls into several categories. There is a local market which caters to the very different needs of the indigenous Fijians and the Indian migrants who form a large part of the population. Much of the differences between the two races and their cultures are reflected in the kind of personal items, food and jewellery they purchase. There is also a thriving market for visitors which offers duty free electronic goods, watches, cameras, perfumes, gems, gold and brand name products from Europe and Asia. Fijian handicrafts and artefacts are the final category and these range from well executed traditional items to carvings and gift items for the tourist trade.

Jewellery

As a general rule, prices for jewellery are cheaper in Fiji than they are in Europe, Australia, the USA and even Singapore and Hong Kong. Much depends on the person shopping as it is often possible to bargain. The feeling of having got a good deal can be most satisfying although how much of a bargain is something only a local

One of the many duty free shops that line Suva town

Gold jewellery is a bargain

expert who knows real values will be able to tell.

As a general guide, a wedding band of 22 carat gold will cost approximately F$50 in Fiji whereas the same ring would cost more than double the price in Europe. One reason for lower prices is that gold in Fiji is sold by weight whereas small items in most other countries are sold by the piece. Precious stones are also cheaper in Fiji; a 1 carat diamond sells for F$14,000 whereas its price in, say, Australia would be more than F$20,000.

Lower prices are made possible in Fiji because merchants often have to consider the local market which is neither large or wealthy. Overheads, determined by rents and labour costs, are also lower in Fiji and the Indian shopkeepers who control most of the industry are prepared to accept smaller returns. Armed with this knowledge, the happy shopper can walk the streets of Nadi, Suva, Lautoka or Sigatoka looking for bargains.

Handicrafts

There is no doubt that you get what you pay for and the choice is formidable. Handicrafts and artefacts include well-made replicas of old weapons, bowls used for ritual purposes and *yaqona,* baskets, *masi* cloth and fans. It's illegal to take out *tabua* (sperm whale teeth) which are of great ritual value in Fiji.

One 500-year-old clay pot was recently found, but rarely are these in mint condition as most antiques are made of wood and therefore prone to the ravages of time. The National Museum in Suva has a fine collection as do some of the old European families, but the museum certainly won't part with theirs and visitors are unlikely to find families willing to sell their heirlooms. What you may find with little difficulty are genuine stone adzes at villages.

Jacks Handicrafts Limited with three branches: the Sheraton Resort (Tel: 700083), Main Street, Nadi town (Tel: 700744) and Sigatoka (Tel: 500810) sell a wide range of products.

Curio shops and woodcrafts

Novelty items, artefacts and handicrafts, books, clothes, jewellery and an extensive collection of Pacific Islands sea shells, including expensive collectors items such as the golden cowrie, are available at good prices.

Electronic Goods

There are scores of duty free shops selling cameras, electronic equipment and perfumes in Suva, Nadi and Lautoka. For top quality hifidelity equipment try **Maneklal's at** 141 Vitogo Parade, Lautoka, Tel: 665242, or its branch at the Honson Arcade, Thomson Street, Suva, Tel: 305384. Maneklal's imports the best brand names and offers a selection of top of the line equipment at good prices. These are generally between 10 and 20 percent lower than in most other countries, depending on the product.

Clothing

There are dozens of clothing stores with an excellent selection of T-shirts and casual wear. Fiji is a major exporter of clothing to Australia, New Zealand and the United States. Prices are low in comparison, even for some of the better quality clothes. There is a very good selection of hand-dyed muslin cotton *sulus*. This is the Fijian name for the wraparound known throughout the Pacific as either *sarong*, *lava lava* and

Cotton sulus

pareo. Prices range from F$10 to F$15 for muslin cotton *sulus* and much less for other types of material. Wearing a *sulu* is fun, and practical as well in Fiji's hot climate.

Municipal Markets

Each town has a municipal market which opens early in the morning and closes at 5pm. These are always colourful and especially so on Friday and Saturday mornings when the markets are at their

busiest with vendors spilling onto the footpaths and even the roads. Fresh vegetables, root crops, seasonal fruit such as avocado, pineapple, mango, papaya and banana, spices essential for Indian cuisine, piles of dried *yaqona* and local tobacco cured into coils are usually on display.

Yaqona (piper mysthisticum) roots are pounded into powder and mixed with water to produce a mildly narcotic drink to which most of the population, both Fijian and Indian, are extremely partial to. *Yaqona* has an important ritual significance in Fijian

Municipal market, Suva

Cassava for sale

culture. An elaborate ceremony surrounds its presentation, preparation and serving. Visitors will have many opportunities to taste it. A slight numbing of the mouth is the immediate effect. It takes a great deal of *yaqona* (imbibing over several hours) to produce a mildly euphoric state. Regular drinkers of the drink are said to experience a quicker response.

Municipal markets offer the best opportunity for absorbing the local scene. Suva has the largest (see *Pick & Mix* page 30). You can stand to one side with a slice of fresh pineapple or melon in hand and watch the press of people without feeling that you're intruding.

Shopping Tips

A word of caution: It can be fun strolling down the streets of Nadi, Lautoka or Suva. The air is usually heavy with the smell of incense, loud Hindi music and the aroma of spicy foods. Sometimes the Indian shopkeepers can be over enthusiastic with their 'g'day mate!' greetings in their bid to try and get customers into their stores. Most visitors take it in their stride but some find it annoying.

Beware of Fijians who seem eager to make friends, especially the so-called 'sword sellers'. Most Fijians are genuinely friendly and it is so disarming that most visitors to Suva, Nadi and Lautoka fall easy prey to the 'sword sellers' who trade on it. The ploy is very simple: a 'sword seller' will first make friends with a cheery 'bula!' or 'hello, mate!' and then proceed with inquiries about your family and country of origin. He will finally ask your name while at the same time fish out a piece of wood in the shape of a sword

Shell and handicraft market

and start carving your name on it, and then demanding an exorbitant sum for this piece of junk. If you should happen to meet one of these rascals on the streets, just walk away. Just keep walking no matter what he says. Do not look back. If necessary, walk into the nearest store and ask the shopkeeper to call the police. There is nothing he can do and you will save yourself a great deal of anguish. Beware also of 'guides' who promise to take you to shops where you will get the 'best' bargains.

Eating Out

Fiji's multi-racial mix is well reflected in the array of cuisines available. Here you will find European food (with a French bias) prepared by leading chefs in the major resorts; Chinese (predominantly Cantonese); Indian with its emphasis on chillies and spices; ethnic Fijian; and a blending of various styles so that a smorgasbord presentation may include some of each.

Fijian Cuisine

The late Ratu Sir Edward Cakobau, as a guest at the Captain's table on his way to England, was clearly not amused when questioned about Fiji's cannibal past. He solemnly studied the menu for some time, turned to the waiter and without batting an eyelid replied: 'The menu does not appear very interesting. Could you please bring me the passenger list?'

Man-eating jokes aside, Fijian cuisine relies on fresh food, cooked simply, usually by boiling. Coconut cream, pressed from the shredded flesh of the nut, is either added during the cooking process or served as a sauce. When the cream is added during cooking, it is called *lolo*; when used as a sauce, it is known as *miti*.

Sunday is always a feast day as in biblical times. Fijians are Christians and punctilious about observing the Sabbath. This day is

Sunday lunch after church

reserved for worship and family get-togethers around a midday feast immediately after church service. Economic circumstances determine the food that is served, but even in villages where money is scarce, the number of dishes will nevertheless be impressive: fresh fish, shellfish, seaweed and *beche de mer* (sea cucumber) from the lagoon, various root crops and vegetables, chicken and sometimes meat, and for dessert, cakes and puddings made from bananas and

Placing food in a lovo

papayas, and fresh fruit. Often there will also be a Fijian version of chop suey and curry. Another local favourite is *kokoda* (fresh, cubed fish marinated in lemon juice and coconut cream) are served with hot chilli peppers.

The *lovo* is a Pacific Islands speciality and an ingenious way of cooking food. A pit is dug and lined with river stones and fire is set on the stones, with more stones placed on top of pieces of wood. The size of the pit and of the stones will depend on the amount of food to be cooked. It may be as large as a small swimming pool where a mountain of food will be cooked including whole pigs, turtles, fish, beef, root crops and vegetables. In former times it was also the principal means of cooking human flesh.

The fire is allowed to die down and the unburnt pieces and embers are removed and the stones levelled. Green mid-ribs of coconut fronds are placed over the hot stones and food, wrapped in leaves but more often in foil, is placed on the sticks so that the food will not come into direct contact with the stones. Banana leaves and sacking are used to cover the pit and soil is heaped over the *lovo* to trap the heat inside. Two hours later, the 'oven' is opened and the food is ready to be served. Most hotels and resorts feature *lovo* nights accompanied by Fijian entertainment.

Recommendations

Apart from restaurants recommended in the itineraries, the following are some of my personal favourites. Invariably, the best food is served at the best hotels. The **Sheraton** and **Regent** resorts at Denarau Island, Nadi, each have a number of

Live crabs ready for the pot

restaurants which serve Fijian, Indian, Chinese and European dishes as well as buffets and *lovo* meals. Prices depend on the restaurant but can be up to F$50 for a main course, though it is possible to have an evening meal for less than F$20. The average price for a three-course dinner for one person without drinks is categorised as follows: Expensive = F$30 and above; Moderate = F$21–F$29; Inexpensive = F$20 and below.

Nadi

THE SHERATON RESORT
Denarau Island
Tel: 701777
Four excellent restaurants to choose from:
PORTS OF CALL
Dinner only. *Expensive*
MALOLO RESTAURANT
Dinner only. *Expensive*
VERANDAH
A sumptuous buffet is served for breakfast, lunch and dinner. *Moderate*
OCEAN LANAI
Lunch and dinner. *Inexpensive*
THE CAFE
Light meals from 10am–10pm. Good food well presented in very pleasant surroundings. *Inexpensive*

THE REGENT RESORT
Denarau Island
Tel: 750000
GARDEN VIEW
Dinner only. *Expensive*
STEAK HOUSE
Lunch and dinner. Superb salad bar. *Moderate* to *Expensive*
OCEAN TERRACE
Breakfast and dinner. The Swiss chef commands a select group of local and expatriate chefs who whip up excellent meals. *Expensive*

COFFEE LOUNGE
360 Main Street
Tel: 701122
Very clean restaurant serving good and cheap Indian vegetarian food. A combination *thali* (platter) includes *roti* (unleavened bread), *dhal, papadam, samosas,* curry and rice. Other dishes are available as well as homemade ice cream in several flavours. An espresso machine serves piping hot coffee. Open daily for lunch except Sunday. *Inexpensive*

CURRY HOUSE
11 Sagayam Road
Tel: 700960
The Curry House serves the full range of deliciously spicy curries, including crab and lobster when available, at prices which begin from F$4.50 upwards. Open daily, from 9am–10pm. *Inexpensive*

HAMACHO JAPANESE RESTAURANT
Regent Resort
Tel: 720252
Genuine Japanese cuisine prepared by two Japanese chefs. Try the value-for-money set dinner. Open 5.30–10pm daily. *Moderate*

CHOPSTICKS AND SEAFOOD RESTAURANT
Main Street
Tel: 700178
Good Cantonese food, with an emphasis on seafood dishes. Open 9am–10pm daily. *Inexpensive*

POONS RESTAURANT
Main Street
Tel: 700896
Superlative Cantonese cuisine served amidst pleasant surroundings. Open 10am–10pm daily. *Inexpensive*

CARDO'S
Main Street
Tel: 772070
Popular steak house and meeting place for locals who patronise the bar for after-work drinks. Cardo also runs the Roaring Thunder Whitewater Rafting operation on the Ba River. Open 6–11pm daily. *Inexpensive*

Lautoka

CITY TAKEAWAYS
15 Malau Place
Tel: 660001
Cheap but excellent curries – which some regard as the best in Fiji – and takeaways. Also serves Chinese dishes. Open 6am–8pm daily, except Sunday. *Inexpensive*

GREAT WALL OF CHINA
21 Naviti Street
Tel: 664775
Good Chinese food and an interesting menu which includes *beche de mer* (sea cucumber) cooked in a variety of interesting ways for those who like to try it. The Chinese believe in its potency and science suggests there is a good basis for their belief as the flesh of this common sea slug is very rich in protein and minerals. The restaurant is open daily from 8am–10pm. *Inexpensive*

Suva

LEONARDO'S RISTORANTE
215 Victoria Parade
Tel: 312968
Wide range of Italian food but also good steaks and seafood. Many pasta dishes (also available as half-portions) and a good choice of vegetarian dishes. Your meal also earns you admission to the Lucky Eddie's and Urban Jungle nightclubs (see *Nightlife*, page 77), all part of an entertainment complex developed by Liam Hindle and his wife. Hindle is a retired geologist who enjoys good food and wine with a passion. As a major importer and distributor of wine through the Victoria Wine Company, Hindle has the opportunity to visit some of the top vineyards and wineries around the world and claims he has the best selection available in Fiji. As many of the top resorts and hotels are his clients, there is a good chance he is right. Open for lunch Monday–Friday, and dinner Monday–Saturday. *Moderate*

PALM COURT BISTRO
Queensland Arcade
Tel: 304662
Attractive outdoor setting in a courtyard with tall palms. The restaurant is located only 20m (22yds) off busy Victoria Parade. Excellent sandwich bar, snacks, light meals and espresso coffee at reasonable prices. Open Monday–Saturday for breakfast through to afternoon tea. *Inexpensive*

PIZZA HUT
207 Victoria Parade
Tel: 311825
Tasty pizza and pasta dishes. Open daily for lunch and dinner except on Sunday when it is open only for dinner from 7pm. *Inexpensive*

THE OLD MILL COTTAGE
49 Carnarvon Street
Tel: 312134
Tucked away from the city centre towards the Government buildings, but worth the walk. Only restaurant in Suva serving Fijian, Indian, European and Chinese dishes. The lunchtime crowd is largely made up of expatriates, civil servants, lawyers from the nearby law courts and tourists. The food is good with a lunchtime selection that allows any number of combinations: Indian, Fijian and Chinese food on the same plate, if you so wish! Open daily for breakfast and lunch except Sunday. *Inexpensive*

CASTLE RESTAURANT
6 Fenton Street, Lami
Tel: 361223
Good Cantonese food in pleasant surroundings. Open daily for lunch and dinner except Sunday. *Inexpensive*

LANTERN PALACE
10 Pratt Street
Tel: 314633
Cantonese food of great consistency makes this one of the most popular restaurants in town. Lunch and dinner daily except Sunday. *Inexpensive*

THE GREAT WOK
Corner Bau Street & Laucala Bay Road
Tel: 301285
Sichuan food, well prepared and served in pleasant surroundings. Lunch and dinner daily except Sunday. *Inexpensive*

HARE KRISHNA VEGETARIAN RESTAURANTS
16 Pratt Street
Tel: 314154 and
37 Cumming Street
Tel: 312259
Superlative vegetarian food – including rice and breads – served in a variety of combinations. Open daily for lunch except Sunday. *Inexpensive*

TIKOS FLOATING RESTAURANT
Stinson Parade
Tel: 313626
Steak and seafood in a former cruise boat moored off Stinson Parade. Open daily for lunch and dinner except Sunday. *Moderate*

LALI RESTAURANT
Suva Travelodge
Victoria Parade
Tel: 301600
Excellent Sunday poolside barbecue. *Moderate*

PENNYS RESTAURANT
Suva Travelodge
Victoria Parade
Tel: 301600
Daily from 6am–11pm for breakfast, lunch and evening meals. *Moderate*

Nightlife

The kind of nightlife you look for in Fiji will depend on how dangerously you wish to live. A drunk is a drunk and can either be a nuisance or a menace. Fiji is a small place and the choice of places to go to at night are limited. There is no national orchestra, no ballet and no theatre. Most large hotels have resident bands and discos and in these places you are likely to see more of other tourists and very few locals.

Locally-brewed beer

On the other hand, nightclubs which cater mainly for locals can sometimes become volatile, as excitement, fanned by loud music, drink and the presence of pretty girls can have unpredictable effects on village boys, often resulting in either fist fights or riots.

Most nightclubs in Fiji will continue until the early hours of the morning, or as long as there is a large crowd present; the exception being Saturday when all clubs are supposed to close at the stroke of midnight because of the Sunday Observance Decree.

Nadi

In the Nadi area, the **Planters Club** (Tel: 701777) at the Sheraton Resort, Denarau Island, stands out. Apart from hotel guests, you are likely to find quite a few of the local people enjoying the ambience. The atmosphere is lively and the security is tight. The barmen are competent at mixing drinks and dance behind the bar while serving customers. The best nights are Fridays and Saturdays when the locals arrive in large numbers.

When the action proves too hot, it is nice to step out and cool off on the edge of one of the pools in the foyer or stroll to the swimming pool near the beach. The **Malolo Lounge**, next to the Planters Club, features a resident band and a more languid pace.

For those who want a taste of the local scene, **Ed's Bar** (Tel:

Hotels often feature entertainment from Polynesia

790373), and **Jessica's Nightclub** (Tel: 790044), at Martintar between Nadi International Airport and Nadi town, are the places to go. Weekends are always the busiest. Ed's Bar tends to attract a more cosmopolitan crowd whereas Jessica's is the haunt of the younger Fijian set. Friday is the busiest night and the action continues till the early hours of the morning.

Although club hours on Saturday are restricted to midnight in deference to the Sunday Observance Decree, often no one pays attention to this and the partying often continues well past the hour.

Suva

As the the largest metropolitan centre in Fiji, Suva's nightlife is the most varied. As with Nadi in the west, the night scene is almost entirely confined to bars and nightclubs. The major hotels, **Travelodge**, **Berjaya Hotel** and **Tradewinds Hotel** are best for casual drinks during the day.

O'Reillys (Tel: 312884) is an Irish pub with a large bar and comfortable seating. It is a notch above most other establishments and attracts an interesting crowd of locals and expatriates. O'Reillys is part of an entertainment complex and includes two restaurants,

the Pizza Hut and Leonardo's Ristorante, and the **Lucky Eddie's** and **Urban Jungle** nightclubs. Both outlets are popular with locals and visitors alike and have the advantage of being situated on Victoria Parade, Suva's main street.

The nightclubs charge a nominal admission fee and drinks are considered inexpensive by international standards. Friday nights tend to be jam-packed, but Lucky Eddie's is busy from midweek onwards. Some of the most attractive people in the world – who represent a broad cross-section of Fiji's multi-racial society – will be gyrating to loud music. You will find Fijians, Indians, Europeans, other Pacific Islanders and every possible combination in between, all having a good time. Visitors can play the interesting game of trying to establish the less obvious ethnic combinations. Fiji seems to have them all: there are part-Europeans, part-Chinese, part-Rotumans, part-Indians and sometimes part-everything!

Dinner at Leonardo's Ristorante earns you free admission to Urban Jungle and Lucky Eddie's nightclubs. This represents a substantial savings for a large party as admission is F$4 per person from Thursday through Saturday, and F$2 on other nights. Suva is not a large city and it's likely you will see the same faces at different spots during the night.

Two other popular watering places are nearby: Traps (Tel: 312922) and the **Golden Dragon** (Tel: 311018) – probably the oldest surviving nightclub in Suva – further down on Victoria Parade. Traps has a similar clientele to Urban Jungle's and Lucky Eddie's.

By 11pm everyone is in place for the duration of the evening. The Golden Dragon attracts its own band of followers but it tends to be less cosmopolitan, unless you count the Taiwanese, Korean and Japanese fishermen whose boats happen to be in port for an overhaul. My recommendation would be to have a late dinner at the Pizza Hut or the Leonardo's Ristorante and then check out Lucky Eddie's or Urban Jungle, or both, for a most pleasant evening.

There are other places but which I would not go if you paid me. Some visitors to Fiji, however, may crave a great deal more adventure and taxi drivers will be only too happy to make suggestions. Good luck!

Nightlife away from the main centres and on the smaller islands is usually restricted to the larger resorts – usually a band with amplified instruments and a disco – but even small hotels usually have a string band and a dance floor. The action really depends on the crowd, so if it's a thriving nightlife you're after, try and pick a resort that attracts a fairly youngish clientele.

Nightlife on resorts is low-key

Calendar of Special Events

Fiji lacks the ancient festivals and carnivals of other parts of the world, except for those celebrations introduced by its migrants like Easter, Christmas, the Hindu festival of Diwali (Festival of Lights) and the Muslim fasting month of Ramadan. Events which may have been celebrated by Fijians before the introduction of Christianity no longer exist. The only exception are ceremonies observed at the deaths of prominent chiefs and the installation of their successors. These survive in modified form and are spectacular to observe. Hotel tour desk staff usually know of such events.

Hindus perform fire walking as an act of faith. Such events are not scheduled and the date is determined by a temple priest. Once the date is set, the event is usually made known to the public. Fire walking is probably the most spectacular of events as devotees – after a 2-week period of preparation which involves abstinence from sexual intercourse and a restricted diet – gather at the nearest river or the sea for ritual cleansing. The celebrants then skewer their faces and bodies with silver pins and while in a trance, march to a temple to walk over a bed of red-hot coals.

Other festivals such as the Hibiscus

Hindu fire-walking ceremony

Festival in Suva in August, the Sugar Festival in Lautoka in September, and the Bula Festival in Nadi in July are of recent origin and no doubt will eventually become part of the fabric of the country in the near future. As dates vary from year to year, check with the Fiji Visitors Bureau (Suva, Tel: 302433, or Nadi, Tel: 722433) for precise dates of the festivals. The Visitors Bureau usually has a list of coming events.

JULY

Bula Festival. A week-long festival with daily entertainment, culminating in a procession of floats, brass bands, marching contingents and beauty queens through the streets of Nadi. Festival grounds have an amusement park with carnival rides.

AUGUST

Hibiscus Festival. This is undoubtedly Fiji's biggest festival. Originally begun as something for the tourists, the Hibiscus Festival is now celebrated as a week of fun for the locals. The festival features a programme of nightly entertainment and culminates in a procession of floats through the streets of Suva and a grand finale at Albert Park on Saturday night when the new queen, acknowledged as Fiji's loveliest, is chosen.

SEPTEMBER

Sugar City Festival. A week of fun in Lautoka in much the same vein as the Hibiscus Festival in Suva.

OCTOBER / NOVEMBER

Diwali. A Hindu festival of lights in honour of the goddess Laxmi. Thousands of clay lamps are lit by Hindu devotees around homes throughout the country as people visit each other and exchange gifts of sweets. Some of the wealthy merchants in town also festoon their homes with displays of flashing electric lights.

NOVEMBER / DECEMBER

Ratu Bilibili Festival (chief bamboo raft festival). This is without doubt

Ratu Bilibili Festival

Fiji's most striking festival. Each year, the people of the Naitasiri province sail on large bamboo rafts, known as *bilibili*, on the Wainimala River to its confluence with the Rewa River and then onto Nausori town where they camp to raise money for their district. The fleet arrives, with more than 200 people, who hold a fund-raising carnival in town. At the end of the day, the *bilibili* are sold to willing buyers who dismantle the rafts for the bamboo used in the construction. The people also bring produce which is sold as part of the fund raising. During former times when there were no roads or powered craft, much of the produce from the fertile Rewa, Wainibuka and Wainimala River valleys made its way to Nausori on bamboo *bilibili*.

PUBLIC HOLIDAYS

In addition to the variable dates for Easter and Good Friday (April/May), Diwali (October/November) and Prophet Mohammed's Birthday, the following are public holidays:

New Year's Day	January 1
Ratu Sukuna Day	May 31
Queen's Birthday	June 14
Constitution Day	July 26
Fiji Day	October 11
Prince Charles' Birthday	November 15
Christmas Day	December 25
Boxing Day	December 26

Practical Information

Airport is the main gateway and has the usual modern facilities. A second airport at Nausori, near Suva, also caters for some international flights with smaller aircraft such as the Boeing 737s operated by Air Pacific and Air Nauru. Buses, car rental offices and taxis are located at the airports (see *Getting Around,* page 85). When leaving Fiji, visitors are required to pay F$10 departure tax at the check-in counter.

By Sea

There are no direct ship passenger services although cruise boats from Australia often include Fiji in their itineraries. Strict laws govern the entry of yachts in Fiji. Yachtsmen must first clear Health, Immigration and Customs formalities at a designated port of entry. Permission in writing is required if they intend to visit other islands. Immigration officials will advise.

TRAVEL ESSENTIALS

When to Visit

There is no real 'season' for visiting Fiji. Australians and New Zealanders tend to favour the months of June, July, August, September and October during the course of the Southern Hemisphere winter. Visitors from the Northern Hemisphere will find Fiji most attractive from November through May when their own countries may be cold and thoughts of beautiful white-sand beaches and warm tropical south sea lagoons are inviting.

GETTING THERE

By Air

Australia is 3½ hours away by plane. There are direct flights to Fiji from Australia, New Zealand, Japan, mainland United States through Honolulu and from Tahiti through Rarotonga. Principal international carriers are Air Pacific, Air New Zealand, Qantas, Air Caledonia International and Air Nauru. Fiji's national airline, Air Pacific, operates non-stop flights from Los Angeles, Australia, New Zealand and Japan to Fiji and the nearby islands of Tonga, Samoa, Vanuatu and the Solomons. Air New Zealand has flights from London and Frankfurt which deliver passengers to Fiji. Qantas offers a similar service from Europe and the United States. Nadi International

Climate and Clothing

Fiji enjoys a tropical maritime climate. Maximum summer temperatures (November–April) average 30°C (86°F). The winter maximum average (May–October) is 26°C (79°F). It gets much cooler in the uplands of the interior of the large islands. Fiji's 'summer' and 'winter' occur in direct contrast to the Northern Hemisphere so that when it is snowing in New York, it is sunny and hot in Fiji. There is, of course, no real winter. A cooling tradewind blows from the east-south-east for most of the year. It usually drops to a whisper in the evening and picks up again by mid-morning.

The mountainous nature of the principal islands has a direct effect on the climate. The prevailing east-south-east trade winds meet the mountainous barrier and deposits rain. This is great for vegetation but not so good for tourists. For this reason, most of the hotels and resorts in Fiji are located on the western or 'dry' side of the island of Viti Levu, mostly within close proximity to Nadi international airport.

December to April is also the time when tropical cyclones from the northwest of Fiji begin trekking south and sometimes pass over the group. The cyclones usually bring winds with gusts of up to and over 100 knots near their centre and heavy rain. There is ample warning from the meteorological office and hotels and resorts are experienced in coping with problems associated with cyclones. Bad weather usually lasts no more than 24 hours. Cyclones do not necessarily occur each year. There was a period from 1967 to 1980 when Fiji recorded only one incident.

Having escaped the wrath of destructive cyclones for 20 years, Fiji was visited by two cyclones in quick succession – the relatively mild cyclone Joni in December at the close of 1992, and the more disastrous cyclone Kina which arrived on the second day of 1993. The resulting floods were the worst in more than 100 years. Tourist infrastructure, built to withstand the winds were not affected, although villages and farmers in the river valley networks received the brunt of the rains.

Visitors to Fiji need a light tropical wardrobe. Bathing suits, shorts, T-shirts and as they will soon discover, *sulus* (known also throughout the Pacific as *pareo* or *sarong*), are a must for both men and women. There are at least 10 different ways in which women can use it, even for evening wear. As the largest Christian denomination in Fiji is Wesleyan (Methodist), visitors are asked to be careful not to offend local sensibilities. Wearing bikinis and ultra-brief trunks is fine at resorts but not when visiting villages or shopping in town. At such times it is easy to take a *sulu* to use as a wraparound so that no offence is caused.

Fiji enjoys a balmy tropical climate

Gleeful Fijian youngsters

Visa and Passports

A passport valid for at least 3 months beyond the intended period of stay and a ticket for onward travel is required. Tourist visas are granted on arrival, free of charge, for a stay of up to 30 days for citizens of Commonwealth countries and nationals of Austria, Belgium, Denmark, Finland, France, Greece, Iceland, Luxembourg, Nauru, Netherlands, Norway, Philippines, South Korea, Spain, Sweden, Switzerland, Taiwan, Thailand, Turkey, United States, Germany and Western Samoa. Nationals of other countries require pre-arranged visas. Tourist visas may be extended for up to 6 months on application to the Department of Immigration in Suva, Lautoka and Nadi or police stations in Ba, Tavua, Taveuni, Savusavu, Labasa and Levuka. It is necessary to have an onward ticket and sufficient funds. Those wishing to stay more than 6 months are advised to consult the Department of Immigration.

Vaccinations

Yellow fever and cholera vaccinations are only required if coming from an infected area. Hepatitis A and B jabs are advised.

Customs

After collecting their luggage, visitors will find two signs: NOTHING TO DECLARE and GOODS TO DECLARE. Those with nothing to declare will quickly find their way to the concourse outside the hall.

Electricity

The electrical current in Fiji is 240 volts AC 50HZ. Fiji has generally three-pin power outlets identical to those in Australia and New Zealand. If your appliances are 110V, check for a 110/240V switch; if there is none you will need a voltage converter. Leading hotels and resorts generally offer universal outlets for 240V or 110V shavers, hairdryers etc.

Time Difference

Fiji is 12 hours ahead of GMT.
When it is 9am in Fiji, it is:

London	9pm	previous day
Frankfurt	10pm	previous day
New York	4pm	previous day
Los Angeles	1pm	previous day
Tokyo	6am	same day
Sydney	7am	same day
Auckland	9am	same day

GETTING ACQUAINTED

Geography

The 300 islands comprising the Republic of Fiji are located in the south-west Pacific between the latitudes 13° and 25° south and longitude 176° west and 177° east. It is an archipelago with the islands scattered across more than 517,998sq km (200,000sq miles) of the South Pacific Ocean. The islands of Tonga, Samoa and Vanuatu are nearby and New Zealand 2,253km (1,400 miles), and Australia 3,541km (2,200 miles) away are also rel-

Cosmopolitan Fiji

atively close. The two principal islands, Viti Levu with more than 10,360sq km (4,000sq miles) and Vanua Levu with 5,535sq km (2,137sq miles), comprise nearly 90 percent of the total land area. Most of Viti Levu is mountainous while Vanua Levu is less so. The highest point is Mt Victoria, which is 1,323m (4,340ft) and is located at the northern tip of the Nadrau plateau in Viti Levu. The plateau has an average elevation of 900m (2,953ft) above sea level. The highest point in Vanua Levu is Mt Dikeva which is 952m (3,123ft) high. The third largest island, Taveuni, is also geologically the youngest and owes its existence to volcanic action from Mt Uluiqalau, which at 1,241m (4,071ft) is the second highest in Fiji.

Vanua Levu

Population and People

Fiji's population was estimated to be 738,000 at the end of 1989. Fijians total 363,000, Indians 340,100 and other races 35,000. The indigenous Fijian people are among some of the friendliest in the world and are so disarming that the first-time visitor often asks: 'Is this for real?' The friendliness is part of the culture which regards visitors as honoured guests. Most people will smile and say hello and invite strangers into their homes and villages. It is important not to take advantage of this friendship and hospitality.

Always reciprocate either by buying 500g of *yaqona* (the powdered root of a plant used for ritual drinking) or food such as canned fish or corned beef. Do not go to villages dressed in brief shorts or swimsuits This is highly offensive to the locals. Despite the overall courtesy and friendliness, it pays to be cautious. There are some who will take advantage of tourists (see *Shopping,* page 69).

Multi-ethnic Fiji

Religion

A multi-racial, multi-cultural nation, Fiji is represented by all the major religions of the world. This is quickly obvious to the visitor who will see Christian churches, Muslim mosques and Hindu temples in the towns and countryside. The majority of Fijians are of the Wesleyan persuasion, but all the other Christian denominations are represented. Sunday is observed as Sabbath with only a minimal number of shops and services operating. Visitors are welcomed to Sunday worship.

Language

Due to its British colonial heritage, Fiji is an English-speaking country, although the two major races, Fijians and Indo-Fijians both speak in their vernacular. Hotel staff are fluent in the English language. The Wesleyan missionaries who

first reduced the Fijian language to a written form were faced with a number of sounds peculiar to the language. For example, a Fijian will never pronounce the letter 'd' as in day. In the Fijian language, the 'd' sound is always preceded by 'n' so that it will be pronounced 'nd' as in Nandi. This also applies to the letter 'b' which becomes 'mb'.

This is always confusing to visitors who will invariably keep mispronouncing many words such as Sigatoka, which is actually pronounced as Singatoka, Beqa, which is Bengga and the Mamanuca Islands when it should be pronounced as the Mamanutha Islands. No wonder people are confused.

The following should be of help.

The vowels are pronounced as in the continental languages. The unusual consonant sounds are accounted thus:

- B is 'mb' as in 'remember'
- C is 'th' as in 'them'
- D is 'nd' as in 'candy'
- J is 'ch' as in 'church'
- G is 'ng' as in 'singalong'
- Q is 'g' as in 'great'

MONEY MATTERS

Currency

The Fijian dollar is the basic unit of currency. It is issued in denominations of 1, 2, 5, 10, 20 and 50 dollar notes and also as $1, 50, 20, 10, 5, 2 and 1 cent coins. Coins of 10-, 20- and 50-cent value are most useful for public telephones and parking meters.

The approximate exchange rate at time of publication is US66 cents to F$1. Exchange rates against all the major currencies are posted each day in all banks, listed in newspapers and displayed at most hotels. There is no limit on the amount of money brought in. Visitors are allowed to take out currency up to the amount imported.

Credits Cards and Banks

Major credit cards are welcomed by most hotels, restaurants, shops, rental car agencies, tours, cruises and travel agents. American Express, Diners Club, Visa, JCB International and Mastercard are represented in Suva. American Express can replace lost credit cards and travellers cheques within 24 hours.

Fiji is well represented by banking groups. These are, Australia and New Zealand group (ANZ Ltd), Bank of Baroda, National Bank of Fiji (NBF) and Westpac. All groups have head offices in Suva with branches and agencies throughout Fiji.

Business Hours

Normal business hours are from 9.30am–3pm Monday to Thursday and till 4pm on Friday. There is a 24-hour bank service at the Nadi International Airport. Most shops and commercial outlets are open five days a week as well as on Saturday mornings.

Tipping

Tipping is not encouraged in Fiji and it is left to the individual to determine whether or not to pay a gratuity. Though tipping is not a local custom, you will find local people tipping. This has much to do with social attitudes as it is a recognition of good service. Fijians ritually exchange gifts of food, clothing, *yaqona*, *tabua*, kerosene and even money during important social occasions, so tipping can be seen in the light of sharing.

Public bus

Bus

Fiji is a small country and the cost of getting about is not great, especially if you choose to travel by local transport. This comprises buses and 'carriers' – vans and 3-ton trucks equipped with rudimentary seating that pick up and let off passengers as and where they find them. Bus companies offer express and normal services. With the express service, it is possible to go from Lautoka to Suva with stops only at Nadi, Sigatoka and Navua as well as at the hotels. Normal bus services will pick up and let off passengers where they find them. Carrier services are usually operate within a confined area. The hotel travel desk will advise. Otherwise, contact Pacific Transport; Suva, Tel: 304366; Nadi, Tel: 700044; Lautoka, Tel: 660499; and Sigatoka, Tel: 500088. Sunbeam Transport; Suva, Tel: 382704; Lautoka, Tel: 662822; and Sigatoka, Tel: 500168. Tour companies offer more luxurious buses – with comfortable seats and air conditioning – at a higher price. Check with your hotel tour desk.

Taxis are plentiful

Taxi

There is a profusion of taxis and there is none of the frustration of some other parts of the world when a taxi is never available when you want it. In Fiji, they come looking for you. Drivers will even approach you on the street. There is a 50 cent flag fall charge and 50 cents for each kilometre travelled, which makes Fiji's taxis amongst the cheapest in the world. Each taxi is required by law to have a meter but many do not turn it on. Insist that the driver turns the meter on when you begin the ride, and if he refuses to comply, step out of the cab. Drivers will also happily make 'deals' for sightseeing and excursions for the day. A quick check with the nearest Fiji Visitors Bureau office or the hotel desk will confirm whether the 'deal' is in fact a good one.

Car

By world standards, rental cars are not cheap in Fiji, due in part to the extremely high rate of import duty levied by the government on vehicles. Rental car companies are obliged to recover a good deal of the cost of the new vehicle within a 2-year operating period before selling the car. It is possible to obtain an all-inclusive daily rate for under F$50 for a small car, but it is necessary to study carefully what is actually 'included'. As in all things, it pays in the long run to stick with brand names and Avis is one of the best known in Fiji for both its service and reliability. The company is represented in most of the leading hotels and at all the major centres, including Savusavu and Labasa in Vanua Levu. Contact numbers are: Nadi, Tel: 72233 (24-hour service), and Suva, Tel: 313833. Avis is also represented at all leading hotels.

Ferry

There are two major domestic shipping lines which service the islands of Ovalau, Gau, Koro, Vanua Levu, Viti Levu and Taveuni. These are Patterson Brothers and the Consort Shipping Line. Both companies operate large vessels and carry trucks and cars. For information, call the Consort Shipping Line, Tel: 302877; and Patterson Brothers, Tel: 315644.

Domestic Air

Air Pacific, the designated national airline, concentrates on overseas flights and

Sunflower Airlines operates domestic flights

leaves the domestic routes to Fiji Air and Sunflower Airlines. All major islands are serviced by internal flights including a good number of outer islands like Kadavu, which is becoming an increasingly popular destination for dedicated scuba divers. Fiji Air offers a special package of F$180 for a return flight to Levuka, Kadavu, Savusavu and Taveuni. It must be one of the best deals around the Pacific considering that a one-way fare to Taveuni from Nadi costs F$116.

ACCOMMODATION

There is no official rating for hotels and resorts in Fiji. Price is the only real indicator although it would be fair to say that the most expensive is not necessarily the best. On arrival at Nadi International Airport and after immigration formalities, you will see a listing of various hotels, resorts and budget accommodations with published rates. The Fiji Visitors Bureau at the airport will help those who have not made prior bookings. Better deals are available through your travel agent or if there is time, in writing or via fax to see what the best offers are. There is no high or low season for room rates, though sometimes specials are offered during the months of February and March.

The following symbols indicate price ranges for a single standard room. Note that all prices are subject to a government tax of 10 percent.

$	=	under F$50
$$	=	F$50–F$99
$$$	=	F$100–F$149
$$$$	=	F$150–F$199
$$$$$	=	F$200 and above

Nadi area

Located on the western side of Viti Levu, the largest island, this area is home to the largest number of hotels and resorts in the country.

SHERATON FIJI RESORT
Denarau Island
Tel: 701777, Fax: 750818
Has 300 ocean-view rooms with balconies overlooking the garden and the sea. There are four restaurants, two cocktail bars and a disco which attracts expatriates and locals on weekends. The room rate includes a full buffet breakfast, complimentary non-motorised watersports and day-time tennis. The hotel is well run and the staff obliging and friendly. There is a large pool, pool bar and beach, and an adjoining 18-hole championship golf course, all-weather tennis courts and a host of daily activities. *$$$$$*

THE REGENT OF FIJI
Denarau Island
Tel: 780000, Fax: 750259
Tastefully understated rooms with Fijian motifs and views of either beach or gardens. A full range of facilities for dining and recreation. Good food and service, and friendly staff. *$$$$$*

RAFFLES GATEWAY HOTEL
Nadi Airport
Tel: 722444, Fax: 720620
Opposite the entrance to the Nadi International Airport and most convenient for transfers. Pleasant rooms and a 24-hour courtesy bus to the airport. *$$*

Mamanutha Islands

The Mamanutha Islands, which feature superb white-sand beaches and watersports, are just 10 minutes by air from Nadi International Airport. There is an airstrip on Malolo Lailai Island which has two resorts. The airport also serves as a pick-up point for boat transfers to other nearby resorts. A sea plane and helicopter service are available for those who wish to fly direct to their island destination. Regular passenger ferries and high-speed water taxis also service the resorts and Nadi each day.

BEACHCOMBER ISLAND RESORT
Tel: 662600, Fax: 664496
Tiny island filled with usually fun loving people. Caters to day trippers, backpackers and the young at heart. Accommodations range from dormitories to hotel rooms and private *bures*. Prices are inclusive of all meals. *$$*

MUSKET COVE RESORT
Tel: 722488, Fax: 720378
Built by Dick Smith, the so-called father of Mamanutha Island resorts. Smith also

built the nearby Castaway Island and Plantation Island resorts. Musket Cove is on Malolo Lailai Island, the only one in the Mamanuthas with an airstrip. Accommodation is in *bures* by the beach with cooking facilities. Restaurant, bar, general store and full range of activities. Attracts interesting people and yachtsmen who enjoy shore side facilities. *$$$$*

Sheraton Fiji

NAITASI RESORT
Malolo Island
Tel: 720178, Fax: 720197
Spacious accommodation in cottages with amenities which include cooking facilities. Full range of watersports. *$$$$*

TAVARUA ISLAND RESORT
Tel: 723513, Fax: 720395
Surfers dream come true. Intimate environment-friendly resort with 12 *bures* and some of the best surfing waves in the world. *$$$$*

Coral Coast

This is a general term to describe the resort area stretching from Momi Bay to Pacific Harbour on Viti Levu. In the days before the new highway was built, the road followed the coast from Momi Bay most of the way. The area up to Korotogo, 6½km (4 miles) south of Sigatoka, is situated on the 'dry' side of the island. There is a good range of places to stay which cater to all budgets. The nearby beach is good for swimming at high tide and for reef walking at low tide. Sovi Bay is only 7km (4¼ miles) away and offers excellent swimming all year through on the southern side.

SHANGRI-LA'S FIJIAN RESORT
Yanuca Island
Tel: 520155, Fax: 500402
Over 400 rooms on its own island with an excellent beach, 9-hole golf course, full range of activities, five restaurants, seven bars and a shopping arcade. If you enjoy large crowds, this is the hotel to head for. *$$$$$*

THE CROWS NEST
Queens Highway, Korotogo
Tel: 500230, Fax: 520354
Individual cottages with cooking facilities neatly arranged on the side of a hill overlooking the lagoon and ocean. Built by the late Paddy Doyle, one of Fiji's tourism personalities. Popular with locals and visitors alike. Restaurant, bar and pool. *$$*

THE NAVITI
Queens Highway, Korolevu
Tel: 500444, Fax: 530343
A pleasant retreat with nice beach, pool and a nearby small island. The full range of activities are available and the staff are helpful. *$$$$*

Pacific Harbour/Beqa Island

This area has long been the playground of Suva residents. It is only 49km (30½ miles) from the city, has the longest beach in Fiji, and the nearby Beqa and Yanuca Islands offer some of the best fishing and diving in the world.

OCEAN PACIFIC CLUB
Queens Highway
Tel: 303252, Fax: 361577
The only resort catering to deep-sea fishermen. Small and intimate with only eight cottages. Full range of activities as well as fishing and diving. *$$$*

MARLIN BAY RESORT
Beqa Island
Tel: 304042, Fax: 304028
Relatively recent addition to Fiji's tourism industry and the first on Beqa island, just offshore from Pacific Harbour where the boat transfers are made. Offers 12 beachside *bures*. Excellent for divers and fishermen. Good food and service. *$$$*

Suva

SUVA TRAVELODGE
Victoria Parade
Tel: 301600, Fax: 300251
Waterfront location within strolling distance of the heart of the city. Good service and accommodations, two restaurants and pool. *$$$$*

Outer Islands

These include the nearby islands of Ovalau, Naigani, Kadavu, Toberua and Wakaya.

TOBERUA ISLAND RESORT
Lomaiviti
Tel: 479177, Fax: 302215
Small exclusive retreat with 12 beachside *bures* built in a style that honours the highest chiefs. All activities and excursions inclusive in the rates except for scuba diving and deep sea fishing.*$$$$$*

Levuka

Former capital of Fiji on the island of Ovalau, only 10 minutes by flight from Nausori Airport.

ROYAL HOTEL
Tel/Fax: 440024,
Fiji's oldest hotel with some parts dating back to 1860. Rooms have ensuite facilities. Lovely old world charm and atmosphere. Located just in front of the municipal market. *$*

Samoan-style accommodation

View of Suva Travelodge

MAVIDA LODGE
Tel: 440051
Quiet, clean and inexpensive. Serves good home-cooked food. Probably the best value in Fiji. Conveniently located on Beach Street, which retains much of its old-world character. *$*

The North

This area includes Fiji's second largest island, Vanua Levu, and Taveuni, which is the third largest. It includes a number of other nearby islands as well.

KON TIKI
Savusavu
Tel: 850262, Fax: 850355
Former banana, copra, pineapple and papaya plantation with a 9-hole golf course, swimming pool, tennis courts, bush walks and ocean-side activities. *$$*

MATAGI ISLAND
Taveuni
Tel: 880260, Fax: 880274
Only 10 *bures* on a 97-ha (240-acre) privately-owned island. The resort is operated by the Douglas family with special emphasis on scuba diving, deep sea fishing and watersports. There is also a romantic tree-house hideout for honeymooners. Beautiful island with a lovely ambience. *$$$*

HEALTH AND EMERGENCIES

Police

The Fiji Police Force is responsible for the maintenance of law and order and control of traffic. Police should be immediately contacted in all cases of crime and also for visa extensions when away from Suva, Nadi, Lautoka and Levuka.
Telephone numbers are:

Suva	Tel: 311222
Lautoka	Tel: 660222
Labasa	Tel: 881222
Levuka	Tel: 440222
Nadi	Tel: 700222
Sigatoka	Tel: 500222
Nausori	Tel: 477222
Navua	Tel: 460222
Rakiraki	Tel: 694222
Savusavu	Tel: 850222
Taveuni	Tel: 880222

Crime

Fiji has a very low rate of crime against visitors but it makes sense to be careful. It is advisable not to wander about alone in any of the urban areas late at night or in the early hours of the morning, especially when worse for wear because of drink. There have been cases of muggings but these are rare. Women should also avoid going to secluded beaches alone. More of a problem are 'sword sellers' and 'guides' who trade on the gullibility of visitors. (See *Shopping,* page 69.)

Accident and Illness

Fiji is free of major tropical diseases, including malaria. It has an effective, western-style medical system although local people still believe in the efficacy of age-old herbal remedies. The Government is encouraging an awareness of the importance of diet and hygiene to health, and for its part, supports the municipalities in the provision of safe drinking water. Fresh water reticulated in Suva, Lautoka and the other major towns are treated and it is generally safe to drink from the tap. This generally also applies to hotels and resorts but not at remote villages. Some resorts use artesian water for bathing, but provide drinking water separately. If this is the case, visitors will be advised.

Hospitals are located in the major centres and there are health centres in rural areas. Hotels and resorts usually have a qualified nurse on the premises and a doctor on call. It is wise to take out a comprehensive health insurance.

Emergency Numbers

Nadi ambulance, Tel: 701128; hospital, Tel: 701128; police, Tel: 700222. Urgent pharmacy, Westside Drugs open Sunday 10am–noon and thereafter on call, Tel: 700310, 780188, 780044.

Suva ambulance, Tel: 301439; hospital, Tel: 313444; police, Tel: 311222. Check with the hospital for the nearest rostered urgent pharmacy.

Lautoka ambulance, Tel: 660399; hospital, Tel: 660399; police, Tel: 660222.

Check with the hospital for the nearest rostered urgent pharmacy.

MEDIA AND COMMUNICATION
Postal Services

Post offices open from 8am–4pm, Monday to Friday at all the main centres. Letters addressed to c/o The Post Office at the designated area will be held for you and delivered on proof of identity. Telegram, fax and telephone services are also offered.

Telecommunications

Coin-operated telephone kiosks may be found outside main post offices. The services are operated by Fiji Post and Telecom, a government-owned corporation. Internal and external telephone calls are easily placed through your hotel which will also arrange to transmit your telex or facsimile messages. The country code for Fiji is 679. There are no area codes. Check with the operator for long distance and international charges, which may also be found in the telephone directory. Most of the major hotels have international direct dial facilities. To call overseas, dial the access code 05, followed by the country code: Australia (61); France (33); Germany (49); Italy (39); Japan (81); Netherlands (31); Spain (34); UK (44); US and Canada (1). If using a US credit phone card dial 012 and book your call with the operator. Dial 022 for international directory inquiries.

Media

The Fiji Times and Post are the two daily newspapers. The government, through the Fiji Broadcasting Commission, operates Radio Fiji in AM and FM frequencies: English (1089AM and 104FM); Hindi (774AM and 98FM); and Fijian, (558AM). Broadcast times begin at 5pm and continue until midnight. Radio Navtarang is an independent station operating on FM96 24 hours a day. Television New Zealand in association with the Fiji government operates a temporary television service in the Suva, Nadi and Lautoka areas. The Government is currently drafting tenders for a service.

USEFUL ADDRESSES

The Fiji Hotel Association and the Society of Fiji Travel Agencies are the two leading tourism industry bodies in Fiji. Consumer complaints should be directed to the Consumer Council of Fiji or the appropriate industry association. Remember to also send a copy of the complaint to the Fiji Visitors Bureau.

FIJI HOTEL ASSOCIATION
P.O. Box 13560
Suva, Fiji Islands
Tel: (679) 302980
Fax: (679) 300331

SOCIETY OF FIJI TRAVEL AGENCIES
P.O. Box 654
Suva, Fiji Islands
(Attn: The President)
Tel: (679) 302333
Fax: (679) 302048

CONSUMER COUNCIL OF FIJI
21 Stewart Street
Suva, Fiji Islands
Tel: (679) 300792

FIJI DIVE OPERATORS ASSOCIATION
P.O. Box 92
Suva, Fiji Islands
Tel: (679) 302433
Fax: (679) 300970

FIJI VISITORS BUREAU OFFICES
Head Office
Thomson Street
GPO Box 92
Suva, Fiji Islands
Tel: (679) 302433
Fax: (679) 300970

Nadi Airport Concourse
Box 9217
Nadi Airport
Tel: (679) 722433
Fax: (679) 790141

RECOMMENDED READING

Cyclopedia of Fiji Sydney 1907, reprinted by Fiji Museum, Suva, 1984, 1985.
Clunie, Fergus. Fijian Weapons and Warfare, Fiji Museum, 1977.
Derrick, R.A. A History of Fiji, Suva 1946.
Lockerby, W. The Journal of William Lockerby, London, Hakluyt Society.
Siers, James. Fiji Celebration, Suva 1986, 1990.
Siers, James. Blue Lagoons and Beaches, Suva 1985, 1989, 1990.
Routledge, David. Matanitu: The Struggle for Power in Early Fiji, Suva 1985.
Williams, Thomas. Fiji and the Fijians vol. 1, The Islands and Their Inhabitants, London 1958, reprinted Fiji Museum, Suva, 1982, 1983, 1984, 1985.

adi	A woman of chiefly rank
bete	A priest-cum-master of ceremonies
bilibili	Bamboo raft
Bula	Fijian greeting, more properly *ni sa bula vinaka*
Bure	Native style house with thatched roof. Many resorts adopt this style but furnish the interior with modern facilities.
bure kalou	Ancient temple
dalo	Taro or yam
kanikani	A condition induced by *yaqona*
lolo	Coconut milk
masi or *tapa*	Cloth made from a species of hibiscus tree specially cultivated for the purpose. The bark is stripped, soaked in water and then beaten out in varying degrees of thickness depending on the requirements of usage. Beautiful and ingenious decorations are then applied to the finished cloth. Sold in curio shops in various sizes. The National Museum has wonderful examples.
meke	Traditional communal dance/theatre
sevusevu	Gift for a guest
sulu	Rectangular piece of cloth
tabua	The tooth of the sperm whale presented on all important occasions, such as births, deaths, marriages, official and family requests etc. No Fijian ceremony of importance can be deemed to have taken place without the ritual presentation of *tabua*.
tanoa	Bowl for drinking *yaqona*
tavioka	Cassava (a tuber cultivated in the tropics)
turaga ni koro	Village headman, usually elected to the post. He is the chief executive of village affairs, overseeing all co-operative tasks.
vanua	Political confederation
vinaka	Thank you; good
vinaka vaka levu	Thank you very much
yaqona	The powdered root of the plant, piper mythisticum. This is mildly narcotic and is imbibed throughout Fiji by all races. As with the presentation of the *tabua*, *yaqona* is a must on all formal and even informal occasions. Visitors wishing to see a village which is not on a tour schedule, should always bring at least 500g of dried, unpounded roots to present to the *turaga ni koro*.

Index

ART & PHOTO CREDITS

Photography
Cover, Backcover **James Siers**
49T **Topham Picture Source**
12, 13, 14/15, 16, 17 **Caines-Jannif Collections**
Handwriting **V Barl**
Cover Design **Klaus Geisler**
Cartography **Berndtson & Berndtson**
Senior Desktop Operator **Suriyani Ahmad**